www. Covenant Friendship . com

by

Rose Mitchell

Jackie,
Thank you for
being a Stepping stone
in the road to where I am
now.
Many Blessings,
Rose
1 Samuel 2:1-2

DORRANCE PUBLISHING CO., INC.
PITTSBURGH, PENNSYLVANIA 15222

CovenantfriendeCharter.net
919-499-3127

For information or to order additional books, please write:
Dorrance Publishing Co., Inc.
701 Smithfield Street
Third Floor
Pittsburgh, Pennsylvania 15222
U.S.A.
1-800-788-7654
Or visit our web site and on-line catalog at *www.dorrancepublishing.com*

Dedication

To Christine

The Godly Woman whose prayers,

love, patience, emotional support,

and sacrifice gave me strength to

keep going when I didn't want to.

Contents

Foreword

A covenant is a covenant is a covenant. Sounds redundant, doesn't it? This is God's way of saying that once a covenant is established, it cannot be broken. It is established for all time and will not change.

God is faithful, and His faithfulness lies in the fact that He cannot lie. If He said it, I believe it, and that settles it. A covenant can also be between two enemies in order to bring peace and harmony to a troubled situation. There is no God but the One True God, the Creator of heaven and earth, who entered into a covenant with man in order to bless him.

The very first covenant was between God and Adam and Eve; otherwise, God would have had to kill Adam and Eve for their disobedience to His instruction not to eat of the Tree of the Knowledge of Good and Evil. This sin of rebellion against God was worthy of the death penalty. There was no second chance—until God provided a way.

The sin of rebellion was worthy of the death penalty. Someone had to die. God in His ultimate mercy substituted a lamb, a sheep, and a goat for the lives of Adam and Eve. This was no ordinary animal that God killed. This was one of Adam and Eve's sheep. One that God had given them dominion over. One that they had watched over. One that they had named. It was not unimportant to them.

The death of the animal signified the death of Adam and Eve spiritually. There was no rebirth, no new birth at that time. Their separation from God was for all time. There was no forgiveness, no second chance. Since they were not expecting to die, this was to them eternity—just as your and my separation from God is for eternity if we do not accept forgiveness from Jesus. Remember, on the cross He said, "Father, forgive them, for they know not what they do." He is our intercessor. He is our High Priest. Without Him there is no forgiveness of sin.

The covenant between God and Adam and Eve is a precursor of our covenant with God. Each generation of people after the garden had to make their own covenants with God, and each time God revealed a little more of Himself. Even today the message is still the same as it was in Abraham's day,

"If you will let me be your God and you will be my people, this is what I will do for you. If you will be my people and be obedient, I will bless you." Are the blessings poured on as rain? Do they come as if from nowhere? No! They are a direct result of letting God be in the driver's seat of our lives and our obedience to His still, small voice guiding and directing us as to which way to go and how to act. Will He continue to bless us? Only in direct proportion to our obedience and our willingness to let Him be in control of our lives. Can we trust Him? Absolutely! He is not a man that He should lie.

My friendship with Rose is a direct result of our obedience to God to go on what we thought was a generic mission trip. Little did we know that God wanted to start something that would bless us for the rest of our lives.

Gwen.

Acknowledgments

I wish to thank God for giving me the desire of my heart in inspiring this book. Because it was His timing and He did the writing it has turned out to be more than I expected.

Thanks to all the persons throughout my life who have been patient with me and helped me grow in spite of all the problems evident in my life.

Thanks to T.R.A., Jr. and Max Dolan for the use of their computers without which editing would have been far more time consuming and tedious.

To Kelly Jo Desjarlais, who took time from her duties as a mom to edit this book.

Thanks to Dr. Daniel Juster for suggesting the name for this book.

And of course Gwen, a precious gift from God who has provided her support throughout this endeavor and graciously allowed me to write about her.

Introduction

The idea for this book was not mine. While I had wanted to write about my military experiences, I had not been successful in writing a satisfactory account of those things. Then one day in the fall of 1995, I sensed God was leading me to write an account of the friendship described in this book. I must say that I did not write this book. My job was to do the typing; God just flowed through my fingers. This is really God's book.

I had originally hoped that my best friend Gwen would write something of her feelings about this relationship, but she felt led to write only the information contained in the foreword. Her statement at the end of the foreword about our friendship will suffice in stating her feelings as she feels that is what God gave her. Trust me, no one, unless anointed of God, is able to handle the many stresses and problems we have had and still remain friends. It has truly been a blessing.

For those who have had many failed relationships, I hope this book will help to explain some whys and ways to change behaviors that have led to failures. The agony I experienced in my failed relationships led to my continually begging God to help me change, and little by little He chipped away at those very hard things and peeled away the smelly onion of my behavior. Those things that made me repulsive to other people no longer exist.

May all of you find help in these pages, for these things apply also to marriages and to those friendships needed between spouses in order to maintain healthy relationships.

This is not all-inclusive; it is only a start, and if you don't start, you will never achieve the beautiful relationship we all want.

Chapter One
Codependency

In her book *Codependent No More*, Melody Beattie defines a codependent as "...one who has let another person or behavior affect him or her and who is obsessed with controlling that person's behavior." That, in a nutshell, is probably the best definition of codependency.

Codependents are controllers and manipulators. They are involved in someone else's business, thinking they are helping. Spouses of alcoholics, drug abusers, overeaters, gamblers, and sex addicts are potential codependents. They try to rescue. Many tactics are used to achieve their goals but few succeed and those rarely. What they do succeed in is causing more problems, digging themselves deeper into the quagmire of depression because nothing turns out the way they want it to.

While I am not going to delve deeply into codependency, I did want to touch on the subject since I mention it several times in the course of this book. However, I do want to refer you to the books of Melody Beattie, which I find candid, revealing, straightforward, and very helpful. Her books contain more information than you will ever receive from many psychologists, and she even gives guidelines on how to start the process of healing for yourself. She also writes from a perspective which incorporates God into the process.

Since I perceive the majority of humanity to be codependent, her books are a way of getting help for the price of a book and not the high cost per hour of a professional.

This book is about my friendship with Gwen and how we have sought to honor God in our relationship. It is a David and Jonathan type of relationship. We both feel God brought us together. Many have been touched by God through us and through our ministering to them together. God has touched others through us as individuals. One of our goals as best friends is to give one another the freedom to be who we are without the codependent intervention I have mentioned. It has been revelatory to me to realize that the more I give up, the more I can have of my friend. How I praise God for the gift of Gwen, who has so generously given of her time, material possessions, and her freedom to facilitate the God-ordained friendship we have.

We have decided that we want a give-and-take friendship. In order to give we also have to learn to take, which is hard for some people. They only see the part in the Bible where it is more blessed to give than to receive. A missionary in Thailand once told me that you have to learn to receive as well, because if you do not, someone else won't be able to give. I also find it interesting that in any successful relationship one must give 100 percent. That means you must also receive 100 percent.

You have to give a lot, **but** you also get a lot. In a codependent relationship the percentages are out of balance.

Chapter Two
A Brief History

My very first recollection of a friend other than family friends is of Marsha. I was eight years old when Marsha and I met on Easter Sunday.

Marsha and I would break the boredom of sitting in church by eating a roll of cherry candy. Sometimes we would have none, which made the monotony of Baptist liturgy nearly unbearable, but we survived. Marsha and I still communicate occasionally. My friendship with her set the foundation for future friendships by giving me a positive outlook on what a friendship should be. She is still a very dear friend with whom I share very precious memories. Had she not moved away we might have been able to develop a closer friendship. Thank you, Marsha, for remaining a friend all these years.

When I was ten years old and in fifth grade, I had the privilege of meeting Julia, whose father was a Baptist minister from Ukraine. She had two sisters. Julia and I hit it off well at first until peer rivalry set in. One of our classmates was jealous that Julia and I were enjoying a nice relationship, and she vowed to break it up.

My parents were having marital troubles. My life was already disrupted at home, so to lose a friend was difficult in an already painful time. In my great immaturity I turned my anger upon Julia and her family.

Suffice it to say that my behavior was dysfunctional at best. It resulted in my expulsion from school, but only after I was paddled by the principal (and appropriately so). I deserved it. Corporal punishment should remain as a part of the school system. It didn't hurt me a bit to be humiliated for my bad behavior.

Little did I know that God would call me to be a missionary to the people of the Russian Republics, and having met Julia ignited a spark in my soul that I have never been able (or wanted) to snuff out. I want to tell Julia how greatly grieved I am that I put her family through such a trial. Many years later, the realization hit me that they had left Ukraine to escape persecution, only to come to the freedom of America and be put through a different type of trauma. To Julia and her family, please forgive me.

After my expulsion I went to another school. There I found friendships in my teachers that have lasted to this day.

My sixth grade teacher, Mrs. Cuevas, was a Hispanic pastor's wife, a woman of God who displayed the love of Jesus. She stands out as the primary example of God's love in a time when I was hurting over my older brother joining the Navy and my parents' marital problems.

Mrs. Cuevas, radiating the love of God, listened to me, loved me, and let me stay after school with her; she even gave me rides home after school. She was my all-time favorite teacher, and to this day she remains a beautiful friend. Thank you so much, Mrs. C.

In seventh grade, Mrs. Bell was my shining example. She, too, was a pastor's wife, and a lovely one. My thoughts and curiosities about sex were coming into play, and she very sweetly put up with questions and hurts that I was experiencing about marriage, divorce, and sex. Some family friends had abused me sexually, and Mrs. Bell became that friend that listened to a young girl's hurts on the subject.

Years later, while visiting Mrs. Bell in her home, she told me this story: "Sometimes I get so depressed and frustrated in my teaching, because so many of my students are slow or have discipline problems (I was a discipline problem, too). At times I want to sit down, cry, and quit, but then I think of you and how far you have come and realize that it really is worth it. That thought gives me the strength to keep on going, that I really did make a difference in someone's life." Wow! What a blessing. Thanks, Mrs. Bell.

Then there was Carol. She and I met at a roller rink and became good friends. If there was ever a close friend when I was growing up it was Carol. We talked about dating and marriage, about boys and how we thought they were cool or stupid. We even made two home movies about boys for one of her classes. (I still have them). We stopped guys on the street and took pictures of each other with them.

Our favorite hang-out was the thirtieth floor restaurant of an office building. We could buy fruit drinks and sit and watch the city. The view over Kansas City was nice, but it made me moody, and I became somewhat reclusive.

In high school there was only one person I could consider, even remotely, to be a good friend. Rhonda was a pastor's daughter who had charisma. She was beautiful and charming. She was probably the girl most sought after by the boys on the ball teams. She would invite the boys to church and fill a long pew with them.

In my first semester of college I met Jan. She was the Homecoming Queen, a popular and pretty girl who treated me like I was someone of worth. Since I felt rather plain, I enjoyed being around pretty girls who made me feel as if I mattered. I was able to build my self-esteem. We are still very good friends. Jan, thanks for being there when no one else was.

Throughout my years in the Air Force there were many nice people but none that I felt close to.

I did not develop friendships with the men I dated. I married a man I had dated for one year, and I found out too late that it is a difficult thing to be married for sixteen years and never have a friendship with my husband. We never cultivated one, and it never materialized. We were both Christians, and I had prayed for a Christian husband, thinking it would guarantee a life without divorce. How wrong I was.

The devil will attack anything vulnerable. Although we had Jesus in our lives, missed very few Sundays, and made sure our children were in church, it did not prevent a divorce. In fact, I felt our Christianity to be a red flag to Satan.

I suggest that when praying for a husband for yourself or for your children, pray for a man of God. There is a difference.

A man of God is more focused on the things of God; a person who is a Christian may be very sincere, but may lack the roots to maintain stability when things get rough.

About one and a half years before our divorce, I said to my husband, "Honey, we need to be friends. We have not ever been friends, let's work on that." His response was, "Don't plan on it, it will never happen." This was only one of the many times his words cut deeply into my heart.

This lack of support and nurturing led to a need to find friends who would help meet my needs. Unfortunately, the needs that were unmet in my marriage were extra baggage in my friendships. Many times my friends did not understand and withdrew from me. This left me hurting, devastated, and taunted by my husband who told me I was not able to hold onto friends. I did not understand this either, which increased my pain and desire to withdraw. However, God in His mercy would not let me withdraw totally.

Because I seemed introverted and very quiet, many people saw me as unsociable. This was not true. Inside I was crying out for someone to love me. I was a wife unloved in my marriage, who felt unloved by those I considered friends. Proverbs 30:21-23 says, "Under three things the earth trembles, under four it cannot bear up: ...an unloved woman who is married,..." I really felt that.

During nursing school Melanie was another married student I became good friends with. We hung out together and talked a lot. Melanie was a bright spot in my life who gave me great encouragement.

Throughout most of my marriage, Theresa, who lived in another state, hung in there with me because God would not let her give up on me. How I thank God for her.

One Sunday in church when I was seven months pregnant with our first child, the pastor said, "Turn around and give someone a hug." Well, Theresa turned around and as my husband watched, gave me a big hug. It felt really good. It was one of the kind that knits your heart with theirs. I immediately began to cry. Something had been touched in my spirit person.

5

A lot of hardness crumbled like the walls of Jericho. I became very dependent on Theresa.

Over the next thirteen years or so I wrote her many letters, made many phone calls, and visited Theresa in her home. She was always a lovely, gracious friend and hostess to a hurting little girl inside a grown-up body, whose husband frequently let her know that he did not love her.

Those letters expressed a lot of intense pain. It was an outlet for me. Theresa felt deeply the things I put in my letters, and I am sorry those things pressed on her. I loved her too much to intentionally cause her any pain.

Theresa was a woman of God in the truest sense. She prayed for me, loved me, and was a spiritual mentor who cried out to God and didn't give up on me. She was obedient when the pressure on her was so intense that she felt she could not take it anymore. She trusted God to work in me. I don't know that I could have survived had she not "stood in the gap" for me. With my deepest thanks for the sacrificial investment, may God bless you a hundredfold, Theresa.

Since the age of ten I have prayed for a "friend who sticks closer than a brother;" the type of friend with whom you can share anything and know it is safe. I prayed for the type of friend who is honest and willing to love you through it all. I had never found that friend. Even Theresa, who was so precious to me, did not feel the closeness to me that I felt for her. It was a one-sided friendship, with me reaping the benefits and her carrying the burden.

If any relationship does not have love, joy, peace, and happiness there is something wrong. Both parties must feel these four things, or the relationship is not balanced and healthy.

Six months before my husband filed for divorce, I met Lisa. Lisa and I became close friends. We prayed together and talked a lot. I opened up the deepest parts of my heart to her as I had always wanted to do. I thought God had sent me that soul sister that I had prayed for for so long.

We did neat things like picnics. I would take my cornet and play hymns while she sang. We loved to shop and shared our time whenever we could.

Unfortunately, she was very attractive to my husband, and God soon told me to break off my friendship with Lisa.

By this time my husband wanted a divorce and because of this I spent four weeks in a psychiatric facility. The pain was more than I could bear.

Lisa is a genuine woman of God; she told my husband that she was not interested in his affections and that she would not mind being his friend, but that was all. She was a happily married woman and there was no place for an extramarital relationship.

God in His great mercy told me in audible words, "Do not seek to restore this relationship." It blew me away, and when I told Lisa, she was devastated as well. The blessing in the situation, difficult as it was, was that she knew this to be correct also. It was not just my imagination.

The hardest thing to deal with at the time of the divorce was not the loss of my husband, but the loss of my friend whom I had come to love dearly in the Lord. This was the time it was hardest to believe the statement, "God has a plan for your life."

When your relationship with your husband has never been good, you grieve over the thing that has been most important and precious. My marriage wasn't anything wonderful, but my friendship was.

Since my friendship was gone and my husband was leaving, I cried out to God, "What do I do now?'" He was very clear that I was to call a former missionary friend who lived in Georgia and talk with her.

She invited me down to visit for almost a week. I went to visit and God worked in me.

She set up healing sessions with her pastor and some friends who for three days and five sessions, laid hands on me and prayed intensely for my healing. I was even delivered from some oppressing spirits. When I left there I had been healed, delivered, cleansed, and uplifted in the Holy Spirit. Wow! What an experience.

While there, my friend, Naomi, introduced me to a group of ladies who called themselves "A Network of Caring Women." The name of this group was Women's Aglow. They were the neatest bunch of Christian ladies I had ever met. They showed God's love in such a way that I knew I wanted to be friends with them.

I flew back home and found there were no Aglow groups available. During this time I asked God what to do, since I was soon to be divorced. He again spoke audibly, "Move to Georgia." I did not waste time getting the job done.

While living in Georgia I made so many real friends, most of them Aglow sisters. These ladies treated me like a sister. Everywhere I go, I look up an Aglow chapter; I have made friends of Aglow sisters in at least seven Aglow chapters. I even know an Aglow sister living in Europe.

I have traveled a lot as a contract nurse since the divorce. At the time of the divorce, God called me to be a missionary to the Russian Jews. This calling has led me to Leningrad, Russia, Moldova, Ukraine (twice), Belarus, and Kosova. I have made many friends in these places also.

On my first trip to a Soviet country, I went with a group who had been invited to go into the schools and distribute a compiled version of the Four Gospels. On this trip I met Gwen.

There are so many more ladies from my past that I don't have time or space to name them. They are no less appreciated because I did not name them or write about them. I love them every bit as much as any other of my friends but this is the story God told me to write.

Before I get to my friendship with Gwen I need to finish with a few more stories.

God is so good about sending us Christian friends and mentors. Our lives are filled daily with those chosen by Him to help us. They are members of the Body of Christ who lend their hands to shape us, use their feet to walk with us, and stand strong to be the backbone we sometimes need. Jean and Betty were two such ladies.

Jean and Betty had always been there for me and in fact, Betty drove me home from the hospital in her '48 Ford.

Jean baby-sat my two brothers and me for years, mostly after school. She came to visit Mom the day Mom brought my brother home from the hospital. I remember asking what gender he was and Mom said, "He's a boy." I then replied, "Take him back, I asked for a sister." My dad later told me jokingly, "I couldn't return him. They told me I wouldn't get my money back."

Being cared for by Jean was an experience in discipline. She was a perfectionist, and it showed when she was teaching me how to do things. She didn't just baby-sit us, we had to work, too! I learned how to scrub the tub, vacuum, and mop. I really hated doing dishes for her, since half of them would end up back in the sink and I would have to do them over.

I was a great whiner and hated to do my homework, but Jean would have none of it. She would say, "Stop that whining and do your work." I could not get by with anything at her house. I am still trying to figure out how she knew I drank the orange juice straight from the carafe.

Sundown is especially nostalgic when I remember it as a child at Jean's apartment. She lived on the second floor, and her back porch faced west. I would sit out there with her dog, Mickey, and feel the warmth of the sun as it went down. Sometimes Jean would come sit with us and she would say to Mickey, "Mickey, you steeenk." How I loved her.

Then there was Betty. Betty had a laugh so warm you just wanted to cuddle up to it. Her home was a haven to me, and many times an escape. In so many turbulent times I would go spend the weekend on her country plot with her chickens, cats, dogs, and her Four O'Clocks. Betty loved flowers.

Betty was an excellent cook who taught me many things. One of them was how to make chocolate gravy. That was before too much attention was paid to calories and grams of fat. She made biscuits and I would butter them up and pour chocolate gravy all over them. What a wonderful breakfast!

Much of my tomboyishness was weeded out by Betty and her daughters, who taught me how to dress, how to curl my hair, and how to care for my hygiene needs when I first started my periods.

Thank you so much Jean and Betty.

How ungrateful I would be if I did not thank my parents for who they were. For so many years I hurt because I thought I had such a rough childhood. Boy, when I finally matured, I realized how very fortunate I was to have the parents I did.

Both my parents worked because they wanted to provide well for my brothers and me. They both worked in blueprinting, and while we did not live in a fancy house, buy expensive clothes or cars, I later realized I had some things that money couldn't buy.

I had a dad who loved me a lot and who never touched me with ill intent. Never have I had to carry incestuous baggage with me. He taught me how important honesty is, and the virtues of not lying, cheating, or stealing.

Mom was a hard worker, a woman diligent in what she set her mind to do. I learned to sew, cook, and keep house. Most of all, she was a woman of God. A woman who, in spite of being born prematurely, weighing only three and a half pounds, toughed it out. She displayed such stamina that most people were amazed that a tiny lady of only four-foot-eleven-inches and weighing only one hundred and five pounds could be so gutsy. She was determined to serve Jesus wherever He put her, and this she certainly did well.

Mom spent her last six years in a nursing home. Dad visited her almost daily, making sure she was well cared for. The last time I visited her, I told her I loved her. In a mumbled but very understandable voice she said, "I love you, too!" We all thought she was unaware of her surroundings.

I just returned yesterday after going back to Kansas City for her funeral. The sweet thing about it was that Mom is with Jesus and I have no regrets. Before I move on, however, I would like to insert a little bit of humor about Mom.

Mom was an avid fan of hot cinnamon jawbreakers. We would always find a bag or a can of them sitting around the house, and Mom was often found with one of them in her mouth. She would take them on trips and play with the grandchildren with one cheek pooched out from a cinnamon ball.

During the visitation at her funeral, my daughter Kathy said, "Mom, I want to put a bag of cinnamon balls in Grandma's casket." Not sure of my Dad's response I said, "I think that is a great idea, but I am not sure what Grandpa would think. Let's ask."

My dad, always the great humorist replied, "It's fine with me, she might even rise up and ask for one." My brother said, "I don't know, she might just pop one in her mouth."

Then there are my children, Stuart and Katheriene. My son and I were always buddies. We have always been close. He is such a tender person. When most boys were embarrassed to be seen with their parents, he would hold my hand in the store. He has been a great comfort.

My daughter is so precious. She married in 1997 and has blessed me with a granddaughter, Kaitlyn Rose, and is pregnant again. She has become a friend as she has grown older and matured. Our kids do grow out of that horrible teen stage and become decent human beings. God blessed me with two very precious and beautiful babies and grandchildren. My granddaughter, Kaitlyn, has inherited her great grandmother's (and grandmother's) love for cinnamon.

Recently my daughter and son-in-law moved away from me. I was devastated. They took my granddaughter Kaity away from me and since I had been with Kaity nearly every day of her life, I was torn apart.

The poem that follows is what I wrote through my tears before they left. I have come into a relationship with a little girl who is "flesh of my flesh" and to tear away that flesh has been intensely painful.

In The Beginning...

In the beginning there was Mamaw.
Taking pictures of all she saw.
First my feet, then my cheeks,
Then the rest of me, in the raw.

It's her face I saw first
After I had seen Mommy and the nurse.
Then Mamaw carried me to the place
Where they began to wash my face,

Mamaw's hands were busy recording me
With those cameras, two at a time, you see.
Video in the left, snapshots in the right,
Mamaw would get her pics or there'd be a fight.

Time to go home, to Mamaw's we went,
That's where most my time I spent.
It was Mamaw who held me close,
Kept me warm, changed my clothes.

Mommy could always count on Mamaw
To watch me when I started to crawl.
Into all, there I went,
That's where my time was spent.

Mamaw helped me learn to walk,
Gave me a chalkboard and some chalk.
On Sunday morning Mamaw dressed me,
And off to church we would be.

Aunt Gwen is Mamaw's friend,
She loved me too, on this you can depend.
I'd yell "Gwen!" then to her I would run,

10

She'd raise me high and give me a hug.

Mamaw would hug me and kiss me so much,
And tell me she loved me a whole bunch.
She'd scrub me clean when she gave me a bath,
Then put me down for a nice warm nap.

Jesus loves me, Mamaw said so,
She proved it by buying me videos,
Kids praising Jesus, I'd dance to it all,
Because, since The Beginning there's always been my Mamaw.

Since the writing of this poem my daughter and her family have moved back near me. Praise God.

Chapter Three
A Picture of My Heart

All my life I had dreamed of one day having a friend so close to my heart that there would be nothing I could not tell her. I began praying for this friend at the age of ten or so. Back then it was more of a yearning to be able to share myself than actual prayer. Prayers came later as I realized that I could actually speak to God and tell Him what I wanted. Some of the things I longed for were not just someone to share my intimate secrets, pain, sorrows, joys, and triumphs but someone who could be honest with me. Too many times people I thought were my friends would be too polite to tell me things to my face because it made them uncomfortable. Lack of honesty in a relationship causes distrust and strife. I didn't want that. I wanted a friend I could spend lots of time with. A friend who had plenty of time to just be with me. I would reflect on little girls who played together, who had all the time in the world.

Memories are a big thing to me, and to be able to make some really special and beautiful memories was a real priority. My friend had to be female because I felt there was a kinship among females men just didn't understand.

I wanted a freshness, a peace, a quality that can only be achieved through a friendship with someone whose heart is directed toward Jesus as her Savior. I was convinced that without Jesus as our foundation, I was just asking for a relationship that was bound to fail.

In several of my relationships I realized too late that the person was not a very strong Christian or not one at all. This resulted in a great amount of pain for both of us because many and great were my expectations, and the failures and rejection were so very difficult to handle.

With the friendships I experienced during my marriage my husband was very confused as to what was going on inside me. He had difficulty trying to figure me out. What was more painful to me was the inability to explain myself, make myself understood, and understand what was wrong within myself. I needed a close friend, a soul-sister. When I finally realized I needed to work with my husband to form that friendship with him, it was too late.

I needed to establish these desires for a Christ-like bond with my husband years before we were married. Praying for a Christian husband was not enough. I needed to pray for a man of God and then begin allowing God to make me a woman of God. This I did not do. How can we expect God to send us a person of God to be our mate if we are not willing to allow God to elevate us to the same level? If that potential mate of God is striving to achieve a goal of godliness and we are not doing our part for that within ourselves, that potential mate will overlook us and not even notice the potential in us. In his mind he has asked for a set of standards that we don't meet.

The same is true of friendships. If we don't set and follow the standards for whom we associate with, we will get pulled down into the dirt along with them and our standards won't mean a thing. Unfortunately, I learned this too late in friendships and in my marriage.

In my search for a friend, I had asked for qualities in them that I had not achieved, hence came the codependency.

I see codependency as having two sides. This is strictly an opinion and not a professional diagnosis.

On one side I see the person who wants to be in control of other people's lives leaving his or her own self unattended. This person needs to take control of him or herself and can't, or won't.

The other side is a person who seeks out people that will do things for them and meet their needs because they want the other person to do it for them. An example is the addictive person who wants to control his spouse and have his spouse rescue him so he can continue his addictive behavior. Then there's the spouse who wants the addictive person to stop his addiction but is afraid to leave him out of fear she will lose control. The thing is, the spouse has no control. Most of these relationships fail, and those that remain intact are a hotbed of misery because the people involved don't know how to resolve their problems.

If you find that what I have written about in this book sounds familiar in your life, do not hesitate to seek some help. There is no shame in getting help. The shame and pain come when you have made some big mistakes and the other person can't cope anymore, and they tell you they are not interested in seeing you or speaking with you again unless you get some help. The rejection is agonizing and painful.

During my marriage I sought counseling several times, and it was beneficial. I tried hard to get to the root of the problem. I did not want a divorce, but marriage is a two-way street. If the spouse is consistently not willing to get counseling as well, change will not come easily.

I also want to encourage you to seek Christian counseling. Our society has its own world-view that does not meet with Scripture. Evaluate the Christian counselor's perspective against the Bible. Some of them do not meet with Scripture either.

Rose Mitchell

One thing that should be eliminated in a marriage is being secretive. Secrets build walls that are difficult to bring down. Engraved on those walls are distrust, bitterness, anger, resentment, jealousy, and many other unseen knives that stab us in the heart.

When I was married, one day my husband said to me that he intended to build a room in the basement where he could keep all the things that he felt were none of my business. In there he would keep anything that made him uncomfortable to show me or to tell me. How I thank God he never got a chance to build that room.

While there may perhaps be a few personal items you may want to treasure, I see no fulfilling purpose in shutting your spouse out of your life just to hog a few mementos that would end up being barriers to growth in your relationship. In fact, regardless of what they are, you or your spouse need to be willing to dispose of anything that stands in your way of spiritual, personal, and marital growth.

Besides, God is specific about secrets. Ephesians 5:12 says, "For it is shameful even to mention what the disobedient do in secret." Guess what! If you try to hide it verse thirteen tells you what is going to happen. "But everything exposed by the light becomes visible. This is why it is said; 'Wake up O sleeper, rise from the dead, and Christ will shine on you.'"

I don't know about you, but to me that sounds as if keeping secrets makes you like the dead. As for me, no thank you. I want to live among the living, not the dead. Plus, when you least expect it, you are going to get found out. Better to confess to your spouse and have him hear it from you and suffer the consequences at that time rather than having them find out from someone else.

Now, there are some things that should never be said. There is a place for secrets, but if you are hiding sin, it needs to be brought forth. Confess to God first, seek His will, and follow His direction. Don't hide something that displeases God because you are afraid of the consequences. Consequences reaped from bringing something forth into the light settle more peacefully inwardly than those which are hidden in the darkness. They may be difficult to experience but God will stand with those whose heart is repentant.

King David, after his sin with Bathsheba, is a primary example. The difference is, David's sin was exposed by God. But when David repented, God was merciful. I would rather take the first step than to have God humble me.

With regard to friendships, secrets can be barriers also. While it is not necessary for friends to tell all to each other, maintaining openness and honesty is of the utmost importance. Shutting friends out can be damaging as well. It can even bleed over into your marriage. No response in one direction of your life goes without its effect in other areas of your life. It's the ripple effect, as when you throw a rock into the water. Make Jesus the priority in your life and you will come out on top in all areas.

Chapter Four
Growth and Healing

This could very well be the most difficult chapter of this book.

How can one explain the complexity of confusion mixed with rejection to have your spouse say, "I've had enough" and divorce you, when he could not understand what you yourself were unable to sort out?

I am sure that if any sense is made of this chapter, it will only be because God has revealed Himself to me in pen and ink, that I may pass onto the reader what I myself have been unable to formulate.

Somewhere hidden inside me, a little girl wandered aimlessly, searching for someone to pick her up and hold her, cuddle her, and speak to her the words of love that children need to hear in order to grow emotionally stable.

My parents loved us very much and provided for myself and my brothers, but it took both of them to do it. My mother, bless her heart, worked endless hours running blueprints, while my dad was the manager of the operation. They were good at what they did, and eventually each of them owned a business location. But blueprinting was not a high income occupation unless you happened to be one of the corporate bosses.

Early in my life, for whatever reason, I grew up feeling a great lack of love. Suffice it to say that our family had our problems; this took away from the time the three of us as children needed to feel emotionally secure.

I was never close to my mother, but she was a delightful Christian woman who always wanted people to know Jesus died for their sins. My dad is a Christian as well and shares Jesus with others. Thank God.

As I began to seek out friends and the friendships became failures, I would temporarily retreat and say, "Never again, God, please do not let that happen again." I would pray and plead with God to do what He had to do, but I begged, "Please don't let me hurt like that again." Then I would go a year or two and get slowly sucked into situations where I could not see that I was becoming emotionally drawn into another friendship that would sap the strength out of the other person and affect her family and mine.

When the person was single, I thought that it would be less of a problem. They had no family to attend to, but then they had school or jobs to deal with. I felt so devastated when the friendship would fail.

While in nursing school, I really liked one of my teachers and finally began to learn to see these things before they got out of hand. One day I went to the chapel, closed the door, turned off the light and got on my face before God. I actually kicked the floor and cried out to God and pleaded, "Please God, no more of this, no more of this. I beg you God. In the Name of Jesus stop this now." I began to see a light dawning, but my struggle was not over and in some ways it was the beginning.

After our divorce, I moved to Georgia to get away from the people and circumstances of the divorce. This was by divine direction. It was one of those profound times when I heard God audibly speak to me.

While there, I needed a boost to my self-esteem. I took modeling lessons, and the teacher was a Christian lady. I again saw what was coming, so I said to God, "I don't want to go through that horrible misery again, so please God, I ask you to help me 'break this cycle of attachment'" I knew of no other way to explain what all that was that I had experienced before.

At this time I shared with Laura, a true friend whom God had placed in my path, the fact that I was taking modeling lessons because I wanted some changes in my life. Four months earlier she had gathered three ladies to pray intensely and daily for me, and sought God on my behalf to do something in my life. Modeling lessons were part of God's response to their prayers.

In asking God to break this cycle, I began to feel a system working in my spirit. When a new response to my modeling teacher arose, I spoke to it in The Name of Jesus and told it to leave me alone; I consciously changed my behavior to avoid what I knew was coming next.

One day I was feeling rather rejected by my teacher. She had other obligations, and I was not able to have the time with her I thought I needed. I left in a huff, and while driving to work I was crying out to God and praying when I saw a vision. My eyes were wide open and I was driving but I saw in my spirit self something that is difficult to describe and painful to write about.

I saw God take a knife and filet my abdomen, starting at my rib cage and cutting down below my navel. What came out was the most awful looking set of bowels that I have ever seen. What was so interesting was that these bowels had names on them: obsession, possessiveness, jealousy, envy, anger, bitterness. I can't remember it all. I just know it was disgusting.

In my mind (because I was still driving to work), I looked down, and, seeing this mass of horrible revelation to my spirit self, I said, "Oh! God! Forgive me please, I am so sorry, please help me God to be rid of this awful stuff and please cleanse me from this evil that you have shown me that lurks inside." I had to endure another nine hours or so before I could go home and repent on my face of the sin God had revealed to me.

When I got home that night, I laid on my face, and cried out to God, begging forgiveness for the awful things that He was showing me about myself. I cannot describe the horror I felt and the repentance I poured out to God. But you know, there was some real healing done with that revelation and that repentance. God was showing me that vision, and in so doing was asking me to obey Him and to repent. I did. There is healing in obedience.

Well, things got better and I felt the strategy of dealing with "the cycle" was working. I actually got a little too confident that it was working too well. I said, "God, I am getting tired of dealing with this, and I have done so well that I would like to just cut off here and call it good enough. Besides, it has been really hard and stressful. Plus, I am afraid the remaining parts will be much harder." He had an interesting answer.

Not in words, but in awareness that I knew was God, I felt Him say something like, "OK. We can do that, but at some point in another friendship you will get about three-quarters of the way into it and you will not be able to finish. You cannot quit and expect to have cured the problem completely, you must finish it." So I said, "All right, God, you win, I will go all the way and finish." The big surprise was that the last one-quarter was a piece of cake, and I have not had to deal with the pain in another friendship like that since.

In a later chapter I will elaborate on the hardships and difficulties I have had in my close friendship with my friend Gwen. They were the acid test to see if I had indeed finished the cycle, and to see what my responses were as compared to previous situations.

I mentioned earlier that there is healing in obedience. When God asks us to obey, He is not punishing us for something or making us toe the mark because He is angry. He wants to heal us. If He tells you to go to your spouse and say you are sorry for an argument, He is seeking an opportunity to heal you. He cannot heal you or your relationship with your spouse, friend, children, or anyone unless you humble yourself and obey.

How about at work when you said something unkind or accidentally bumped into someone? If you say nothing, hard feelings lurk inside and no healing takes place. God wants all of His children to obey.

In the Foreword of this book, Gwen states that she and I were obedient to go on a mission trip to Russia. To me it was the dream of a lifetime, but for her it was a tough thing. She's not one to want to go halfway around the world. She decided to be obedient to God, and wonderful things have come from her obedience.

This summer (1998) I will be making my fifth trip to Russia. I am going back to Kiev, Ukraine, because that is my calling. If I don't go, I may become sick in spirit (or maybe in body); then I would have to seek God all over again to be healed. I'd much rather go before I get sick.

Sometimes though, there is someone else's healing in your obedience. By my yielding to God, we will give medicine, love, and eyeglasses in the Name of Jesus. The best healing will come when we give them the Word of God. I don't want anyone to go to hell because I did not share with them the good news of Jesus because I stayed comfortable in America.

Someone WILL be healed by your obedience.

Chapter Five
The Meeting and the Promise

Gwen and I first met at John Kennedy Airport in New York City. We were with a group of people waiting to fly to Leningrad, Russia (since renamed St. Petersburg) for a missions trip to the schools. I never expected to meet someone who would become my best friend; rather, I expected to find a husband.

When we got to Leningrad, got settled, and began our trips to the schools, a strange thing happened. Either Gwen and I, her friend Deb and I, or all three of us would be picked to team up for the schools. At the end of the day we would all end up in their room or mine for times of sharing and praise.

In the process, I was able to open up and share things that I tell only to a close friend. They also shared things from their hearts. Times of rejoicing would follow. We would pray and the presence of God would come. We were truly blessed. After a few days we were nearly inseparable.

We sat together when we went to church. I remember telling Gwen a joke, and she had a hard time stifling her giggles. The services were so long and boring that I had to do something.

Gwen and I sat through a beautiful production of Swan Lake by the Kirov Ballet. I was elated when I saw the pictures I had taken. Some were taken without a flash (they did not allow flash pictures in the ballet) and they turned out beautifully. I was also impressed that the entire audience was very respectful. No whistling, quiet when expected, and applause when appropriate. Just as I was taught when I was growing up.

Sunday afternoon led us to the summer palace of Czar Alexander at Pushkin. They were sweet times of getting to know someone under the plan of God.

I am amazed that at times Gwen is so spontaneous in responding to God. For instance, in downtown Leningrad near Nevsky Prospect we had just come through an onslaught of gypsies begging money (my camera flash was nearly stolen) when a gypsy boy confronted Gwen. At this point she was several yards ahead of Deb and one of the men in our group. The child was very persistent, so Gwen immediately stopped, laid her hand on the child's head and began to pray for him. When Deb and Don arrived they joined in the prayer.

Finally, the boy looked puzzled, realized he was not going to get any money, and ran away. I believe he got more than money that day. It would be interesting to know just what impact that prayer will have on his life.

The teachers in the schools were so appreciative that we had come to their schools to see them that they would hold tea parties for us and give us gifts. They sacrificed a great deal to give us these rarities. Teachers and students alike would come to us and take hold of our arms and tell us how much they appreciated our coming. One little girl came to me and gave me ten kopecs. It took five kopecs to ride the bus. It must have been a great sacrifice for her.

In one classroom, I stood aside as the other person on our team spoke. On this particular outing I was paired with one of the men from our group. As I stood there, I felt the Holy Spirit weigh heavily upon me, and I could not figure out what was happening. For some reason, I was not allowed to speak, for we were running out of time.

As we turned toward the door we walked past the end of the rows to exit the rear door. I had a strong urge to touch the faces of the girls as I passed them. They had been kind to us, and so generous. As I reached the fourth girl I noticed that she had a severely disfiguring skin rash; I sensed in my spirit God was saying, "Do not hesitate to touch her also." Later I asked God what all that was about and the answer I got was something like this: "I wanted her to know the God you were representing loved her so much that her disfigurement didn't matter." God's power is so awesome.

On the return trip the three of us sat in the same row. We were several hours out from JFK, and Gwen and I were talking about the blessings of the trip. We talked of how we seemed to be able to relate to each other, and of how we could share our innermost thoughts without reservation. Gwen leaned forward a little and turned to me, looked me straight in the eye and said, "You are just like my soul sister." That is all she had to say. I had prayed for thirty years for a friend like that, and most of the time I had used that same term in asking. My God is awesome, and it is just like Him to give us a gift that is not only timely but filled with such wonderful experiences as those in Russia.

When I got home, I said to God, "I don't want anymore hurts or failed friendships. I would much rather do without. I want a friend who will always be my friend. And God, I will try very hard to do the same."

Within a few weeks during our conversations on the phone, I told her that I wanted to base our friendship on Jesus first, then promise to be honest in all things even if it hurts us. I had many people in my life who were uncomfortable with honesty, even to the point of allowing themselves to hurt unnecessarily because they were unable to speak the truth. I was not willing to experience that again.

She was very agreeable to this, which made me happy. And I am so pleased to say that it wasn't as difficult as I thought it would be. But you know, the biggest precaution that is needed when being honest is timing. If your friend is going through some family difficulty, it is probably not the time to remind her that it is February and she still has her Christmas ornaments up. When dealing with my teenager, I did not need her to tell me I was doing something she thought was in error. Timing is of the utmost importance; listening to God is an essential element in when to say what could be said another time.

We have made honesty a priority. In promising to be honest we made a covenant, a pact, a promise, a solemn oath, an agreement to protect the honesty and integrity of our friendship. Later, we made a covenant of friendship.

God made covenants of friendship with Abraham, Moses, and David among others. Jonathan made a covenant of friendship with David.

In 1 Samuel 20:6 David said to Jonathan, "As for you, show kindness to your servant, for you have brought him into a covenant with you before the Lord." 1 Samuel 20:17 says, "And Jonathan had David reaffirm his oath out of love for him because he loved him as he loved himself." And in verse forty two of the same chapter, "Jonathan said to David, 'Go in peace, for we have sworn friendship with each other in the Name of the Lord' saying, 'The Lord is witness between you and me...'"

When David learns of Jonathan's death, David writes a lament in his great grief. 2 Samuel 1:26 says, "I grieve for you, Jonathan my brother; you were very dear to me. Your love for me was wonderful, more wonderful than that of women."

The reason they loved each other so much was because their friendship was based on loyalty, faithfulness, integrity, honesty, Godliness, protection, and genuine love for each other. These two men truly had a God like love for each other. I personally don't see how David handled the loss so well were it not for God sustaining him.

It is scriptural to make covenants with friends, but I think it is a serious decision and should be considered wisely. Had I made covenants with other people in my past, I would be bound to them under this oath; because this is a promise and must be taken as a great commitment.

Numbers 30:2 states, "When a man makes a vow to the Lord or takes an oath to obligate himself by pledge, he must not break his word but must do everything he said." Ecclesiastes 5:4-7 says, "When you make a vow to God, do not delay in fulfilling it. He has no pleasure in fools; fulfill your vow. It is better not to vow than to make a vow and not fulfill it. Do not let your mouth lead you into sin. And do not protest to the temple messenger, 'My vow was a mistake.' Why should God be angry at what you say and destroy the work of your hands? Much dreaming and many words are meaningless. Therefore stand in awe of God."

A prime example of how seriously God holds to covenants is in Joshua, Chapter nine, when Joshua is deceived by the Gibeonites and makes a covenant that they would not kill them. Three days later God reveals to them what they had done, but it was too late to change. Then later, in 2 Samuel, Chapter twenty-one, the Gibeonites are avenged because of the oath Joshua had made years earlier. Saul had apparently killed the Gibeonites, and the price paid by Saul for this slaughter (although he was already dead) was the killing of his descendants. If you make a promise to God or before God, someone will be reaping the results years after you are gone.

Some people might think that the vows God is talking about here are those directed to Him only and those of people getting married. They are only a part. The Word also says to "Let your yes be yes and your no be no."

The Word applies to friendships also. If your word is not good to your friend, your neighbor, your coworkers, and others you meet, why should they trust you? If you can't keep a promise to others, you won't keep one to God.

I know without a doubt that God has held me accountable for the promises I have made to my friend.

Occasionally, even when I was not listening to God, He managed to get my attention. He spoke to me about these covenants I had made with my friend.

On several occasions, I have become frustrated and wanted to quit being friends. These times were painful and seemingly unbearable. Not really wanting to hear from God at these times, I said to Him, "God, I want to quit. I am tired of dealing with this situation because it causes me to hurt and I am unable to control it. I want out!" What He would say I didn't want to hear: "You can get out if you want to, but if I send a husband, are you going to quit him? Isn't your word any good? You have not just promised to your friend these things, but you have sworn them before Me. What about the promises to be faithful and serve Me? Will you break them, too? Is your word no good?" He could have slapped me and not hurt me or impacted me any more.

I have kept my promises to God and to my friend. I really do want to remain faithful in all things.

Our friendship has been a great blessing, and I have stayed with it. I have never been a quitter. The same was true with my marriage; I kept my vows there also. To be known as a woman of my word, first to God, then to humanity, has been a continual goal. It is imperative that we are careful who we make promises to and what they relate to, for God will hold us accountable.

On several occasions Gwen and I have said that being honest has been one of the greatest blessings in our friendship. It gives us the freedom to be ourselves and to enjoy the company of each other. Dishonesty causes stress, hard feelings, lying, and deceitfulness, among many other things.

Also, honesty does not indicate that you have to tell a person everything. One must evaluate the consequences of that information and what it will do.

There will be things that you will never tell your friend if you truly love them. That is where listening to God and knowing what to say enters in. If something will hurt your friend, don't say it.

If you should mess up and say something that you should not have said, your friend should forgive you. God tells us to forgive. If she does not forgive you immediately, perhaps she will later. If she never does, all you can do is ask God to forgive you. If she never forgives, probably she was not your friend to begin with.

Several years ago, before I knew Gwen, I knew a lady that grew fond of me and told me a personal item about herself. I told that item to my neighbor, and God convicted me of it. I felt then I needed to confess my sin to her so that my heart could be healed. It says in James 5:16, "Therefore confess your sins to each other and pray for each other that you may be healed."

I went to that friend and confessed. She was greatly hurt but she forgave me, and I felt reconciled. We must be careful about our mouths. See also James, Chapter three.

Matthew 12:35-37 says, "The good man brings good things out of the good stored up in him, and the evil man brings evil things out of the evil stored up in him. But I tell you that men will have to give account on the day of judgment for every careless word they have spoken. For by your words you will be acquitted, and by your words you will be condemned."

Proverbs 18:21 says, "The tongue has the power of life and death, and those who love it will eat its fruit."

Your relationship with your husband can be blessed by making covenants. Your marriage vow is a covenant but to make a pledge of honesty and friendship can greatly enhance your relationship and help it grow.

Gwen's marriage has been blessed by what she has learned in our friendship. There are aspects of her marriage that I wish to apply in my life if I should marry again. I have learned how to be a friend, and I can apply these principles to my family and potential mate. It has been a proving ground for my responses which I had not learned in my marriage. Had I been more honest and more of a friend, I might still be married.

God is awesome. He is a God of new beginnings. He does not stop with us when we fail. He will still use us. That is why He renewed my missionary call after the divorce. He didn't throw me away.

There is no substitute for honesty and trust in a relationship, whether it be a marital relationship or a friendship.

My friend has a difficult time trusting people. Many circumstances over the years have left her wary of whom to trust. I don't trust men very well. I don't like talking to some men, and would prefer not to deal with most men.

Throughout my life I have been teased by boys and men and have been mocked, most times mercilessly, because of my clothing, my looks, and my personality. Not trusting men comes naturally. It has been hard to trust God because I see Him as a male.

Trust in a relationship is imperative if the relationship is to survive.

Unfortunately, many relationships falter, and unfaithfulness can sneak in; however, with the help of God things can be reconciled. It is those relationships not founded on Jesus Christ that fall apart.

Had we not promised to be honest and not begun to trust, we would have had a difficult time learning from one another. If there is no honesty and trust there is deceit and betrayal.

Gwen and her family vacation occasionally and I have been blessed with the responsibility to keep an eye on their home. In so doing, I heard an inner voice say something like: "Wouldn't it be interesting to see what neat stuff they have in their house!" My response was out loud and to the point. "I rebuke that in the Name of Jesus." Then I said to God, "Lord, my friend has trusted me with the privilege of keeping an eye on her house. If I snoop, I will have to confess to you, Lord, of my sin of snooping and then to her of my betrayal of trust. I don't want to have to tell her that I had snooped." I finished my door checks and then left.

There is no doubt in my mind that she would have forgiven me, but I am not sure she would have trusted me anymore. I have found favor with her so many times that I treasure the long-term blessing of her trust and favor as opposed to a few minutes of betrayal.

Chapter Six
Hard Times and Memories

Although the blessings have far outweighed the problems, difficult times have been very painful when the problems were a result of loneliness.

One of the things I struggle with and find most difficult to communicate to my friend is how to tell her how lonely I can get. Because she has family around much of the time, she is able to cherish the quiet times which are part of her personality type. I am not like that.

On many occasions I have tried, and I feel, failed, to get across to her just how lonely life is for me. It is hard to convince someone who loves solitude that solitude can be boring or painful. Really, why I feel so compelled to make her understand is a mystery. I have asked God many times, "Why is it so important that I make her understand? Even if she did understand, Lord, that probably would not make her any more able to do anything about it. Why?" I seem to get no answers. At any rate, the need is still there, and I try to give it to God. Sometimes I think He must be listening to someone else. In reality, I know better.

During the years I prayed for my soul sister, one of the things I prayed for was someone with whom I could spend a lot of time. Somewhere in those years of praying, I picked up the idea that in order to be close one had to spend a lot of time with that friend, and it would be wonderful. It didn't occur to me that the time demanded by such a concept could be hard on the family life of that other person. Fortunately, God is so good and so gracious that He gave me a friend who is a stay-at-home wife and mom who was able and willing to spend time with me. It was a need that He so wonderfully planned for in this friendship. Thankfully my friend's husband has been kind, patient, and flexible. We have spent a lot of time together. Thank God, He gave me a creative friend who has helped prevent those times from becoming overwhelmingly boring.

Gwen is very happy working in her yard and loves to keep a pleasant external appearance to her home. (The inside isn't so bad either.) Pansies, azaleas, hollies, roses, petunias, and many other types of flowers adorn her lovely property. In fact, when I bought my house she decided to help me improve the appearance of my home. Many are the memories I have of shoveling manure, spreading mulch, digging shrubs, painting my bedroom, and simply sharing chores at her house and mine.

For Christmas one year Gwen felt I needed to start a set of china. I didn't have any, and she wanted to buy me my first place-setting. For a woman, china is a special thing. I am pleased that God chose her to help me get it started.

Making memories is an important part of a relationship regardless if it is a friend, husband, child, or whoever.

We share a mutual friend, Kim, who has a lovely yard. She finds it quite wonderful that Gwen is willing to give freely to anyone who will come and get horse manure. We have made several trips to Gwen's barn on Kim's behalf.

Another favorite memory is the time we worked in her vegetable garden. It was very hot and we were sweating. Gwen said, "Hey, Rose, let's go swimming". I was certainly ready but I had no swim-suit. Before I knew it she jumped into the pool fully clothed and I then followed. Spontaneity is fun.

We have shopped, gone to Women's Aglow conventions, had lunch, put up Christmas decorations, made chocolate Easter eggs, and cut up downed trees from Hurricane Fran.

When I turned fifty in the year 2000, Gwen had a surprise party for me which turned out not to be much of a surprise.

I thought we were going out to lunch before I had to work the three till eleven o'clock shift. I didn't have anything to do, so I showed up at her house early and found her daughter and a friend setting two tables with the best china and crystal. At first I saw only four plates, and thought it was going to be Gwen, her daughter and friend, and me until I walked into the dining room and said, "I guess I must be really early." She then said to me, "I am so glad you came early, I am late and I need to be rescued." So I helped her finish the preparations.

Since it was my fiftieth, Gwen, her daughter, and her friend all served in black. Several other people wore dark clothing to commemorate my being "Over The Hill." We had black balloons and chocolate cake.

I don't accept the negative implications of wearing black, but it was a beautiful memory by a very special person. She even included my entire Sunday School class, my daughter and granddaughter (who told Gwen the chicken was "Good hamburger, Gwen"), and another very good friend.

Holidays are family times. While I have family, they live hundreds of miles away (except my daughter Kathy, and her family). Kathy usually spends some time with me, then goes to her in-laws.

Thanksgiving and Christmas are most difficult for me, because I have the expectation that these are times for people who are close. It is unrealistic to hope that I could be included in these times with my friend on a consistent basis.

Near the year's end when the holidays are approaching, I begin to struggle with knowing most of my time will be alone. I am sure this is true for thousands of other single people or those separated from loved ones.

There are several things to remember when having to struggle through this situation:

1. Remember that your friend is always your friend. Not being able to attend a function with them is not an indication that they are rejecting you, but that they have to respect the wishes of their family members. The other members are busy trying to live their own lives and are not necessarily thinking about inviting non-family members.
2. Don't let the exclusion ruin your holiday. There are others who have it worse than you. I am trying to learn to have a peaceful day alone, and I want to learn the lesson God is trying to teach me.
3. Volunteer to help serve meals, deliver packages, or go caroling. There is usually something you can do.

The devil can have a heyday with your emotions about the holiday season if you let him. He wants you to get bent out of shape in order to ruin the atmosphere for as many people as possible.

If this is a struggle you encounter yearly, start praying immediately that God will not allow the enemy to play with your emotions. Invoke some spiritual warfare. Also, check into the possibility that you may need some help overcoming codependency.

If you find you are unable to do without your friend, you may be in great need of emotional help. It is not shameful to seek professional help for this. Again, I would recommend Melody Beattie's book *Codependent No More*. Believe me, you can overcome this.

Sundays are another time that can bring anxiety into your life. When I was married I always made a roast for my family. This was a time we all could enjoy each other and discuss the week, our jobs, what was important to our kids, and anything that concerned us. I have been single now for over fifteen years, and most Sundays I am alone. This can be an intensely lonely time.

When I arrive home, I will have come from worshipping at church with my friend and her family, walk out of the church and see them and other families going home or out to eat. While my friend has invited me a few times, I would not be welcome to dine with them every Sunday. They, too, need that time of family fellowship that I once experienced.

Almost all my life I have lived for thrills. I have traveled a lot and done many things, but when quiet times come I am not always ready for them.

Sometimes, but not always, I am able to tolerate the loneliness. When I get lonely, I want to seek out my friend. Many times that is not possible.

So, when those times come, I have the knowledge that the only person I can trust and turn to is the Greatest Friend on earth and that is Jesus. But you know, entering into quiet time and that presence is not always thrilling, or easy, and it is sometimes boring because God does not always answer in ways that generate a thrill. There have been times I have sat for hours waiting for the sign like Elijah waited for in the storm or the wind. God may just answer in the quiet of the moment with...quiet. Sometimes, to me, that is not what I want to hear. In those times, the heart knowledge sometimes eludes me.

However, we must not neglect those times or forsake them. They can be most valuable, but I just know that God does not waste anything.

There is always a positive side to everything. Not being married or having kids around can be a blessing, and can be quite peaceful when you do want to. I don't have to share my money with anyone but God, or who He tells me to. The TV is mine when I want it. The car is always there and not out with one of the kids. When Kathy moved out she took the dog and I don't have to feed it or let it out. It costs less for food and utilities. No more school expenses. There's a lot to be thankful for.

The bottom line is: I can always lean on Jesus. He can handle my problems and maybe my friend can't.

Chapter Seven
Growing Up Together

As I look back, I feel there was so much I missed in my childhood. We lived in rough neighborhoods until I was thirteen. My high school was loaded with kids from upper class families and, while some were nice to me, many were cruel.

So I feel as though I lost a lot in growing up. Our Girl Scout leader was wonderful, but older, and lacked the energy of a younger leader. However, she was excellent at arts and crafts.

Along with wanting to have that close-knit friend, I longed to share those growing up times that children are supposed to have.

When my friend and I began to grow in God, He showed me that I was not going to miss that childhood. He was going to help me grow up with my best friend. I suppose I didn't realize that in growing up there had to be tough times as well.

Many of the lessons we have learned have been learned together at the same times; only our circumstances differed. We have been able to cry and laugh at these times, but most of all we feel the intensity of the pain the other felt.

One such time came recently. Although we are very close, I still say things in unguarded moments, that later I wish I hadn't. I have a great desire to protect her, but there are times I let my guard down and say something cutting. I did that recently. Thank God for our honesty even when it hurts.

She began to share with me about how much I had hurt her and that it even felt like a wedge coming between us. The grief that filled my heart over the pain I had caused her made me numb for over a week. Several days we did not even speak. Neither did we call. I just had to keep seeking God. Oh, how I have prayed and repented.

When I asked God what I needed to do to correct what I had done the only thing I got was "Wait on Me." When He finally spoke to me, His answer was, as always, interesting.

Remember the little girl from Ukraine? When I realized I hurt her I was greatly grieved that I had said and done things to hurt her and her family. While all these years I have wanted to apologize to her I never saw her again, and so I have carried this hurt with me since.

God showed me that I was only seeing and feeling the hurt from my perspective. I had not been close enough to her to really feel the pain coming from her. I was not able to share her pain, so I really did not know how bad she felt.

In this recent incident with Gwen and the realization of the depth of hurt I had caused her, I began to see the other little girl whose pain was just as great. I couldn't see it before. Seeing the pain in my friend now touched me in a place not ever touched before. I was feeling that until I felt the pain of the Ukrainian child, I could not heal from it, nor could I see the pain I had caused my current friend and heal from it.

To some this may sound like gibberish but until I realized the depth of pain my Ukrainian friend felt, I could not effectively meet her again and reconcile that relationship. I would have been only thinking of my own pain and not of hers.

I didn't expect that growing up was going to be this difficult.

Chapter Eight
Respecting Authority

Since I have found such precious Christian fellowship and knitting together of our hearts as friends, I never want to lose that beautiful gift that God has blessed us with. When you want something so badly you will do anything for it, you will seek to find avenues to make it better so that it may be preserved. You will do almost anything to protect it.

Not long after we began our friendship, I found out in a way I never realized what I would have to do to ensure the continuation of our friendship.

One of the points of this book is that my friend is married. She has a responsibility to her family. Scripturally speaking, that is her first priority; I am impressed at the Proverbs 31 example that she presents. She literally has bought fields, she plants gardens, she is well respected in the community and at church, she gives of her time, talents and resources to benefit other people, and she holds offices in church and auxiliary functions. I also find in her the dignity and honor of a Godly woman. She has a strong desire to be kind and to associate with those whose lives exude kindness. She is a "Southern Belle" in the truest and most honorable sense of the term.

I realized that because she was married, I was not going to have a friend who could spend *all* the time with me that I prayed for. I have been abundantly blessed in that area nevertheless. Not only was that an unrealistic expectation to begin with, I myself have not had as much time to spend with her as I would like. I also have children.

If I am to be Gwen's friend, I must yield to the authority of her husband. I have a problem with men having authority over me anyway, because of some very painful experiences, including my marriage. The Lord showed me that His plan for a family is for the man to have a desire to protect and defend his family. Anyone who appears to be a threat causes him to sit up and intervene when he senses danger.

Also, God revealed to me early on that if I intended to cultivate and yield fruit in this friendship, I needed to cultivate and yield fruit in a friendship with her husband. This does not necessarily mean in the same depth and personal way as with her, but that I must show scriptural respect and yield deference to his authority.

For instance, if she and I make plans to have lunch and he calls wanting her to have lunch with him, I am obligated to give way. I cannot have an attitude and say, "We have already made plans and this is not fair!" As much as it may hurt, I must yield.

I am not saying it would be right for him to sabotage our plans, but there are times when I have to stand back and say, "Okay let's try tomorrow or the next day." In fact, she and I have worked it out to about once a week. So far that has been acceptable, and her husband honors our arrangement.

As her friend, I come under his authority in the sense that if I want peace in our friendship, I had better let him have the say in his family.

One thing that God showed me years ago which was quite revelatory was in the relationship of a coworker and her best friend. God showed me the effect of being too codependent on your best friend.

When living in another state, I had a coworker who had a room in her best friend's home. This lady was single and her friend was married with two children. God got my attention and I watched the outcome of the situation with great interest. It put great stress on the family's privacy and on the relationship between two friends. The single girl eventually moved out, but by that time the couple were having marital problems.

While I have no plans to move into my friend's house, I learned a great lesson from that situation long before I knew Gwen.

This does not mean I am totally happy with some of the decisions her husband has made, but I respect his authority over her. He could make or break our friendship. If she were pressured into a position to choose, I would lose.

Since I have had the need to express my feelings in this area, I can be honest with her. That honesty releases tension and anxiety.

It is very important that you not speak down to, talk trash about, or set about to discredit your friend's husband. They are one flesh, and you would be speaking against your friend. Some people tend to associate opinions inclusive of the entire family. Gwen's husband and I work in the same place. If I were to gossip about them, I would not be perceived by others as a friend; thus I could not be a friend to others.

I have heard people say things like, "Suzy is my best friend, but her husband is a real jerk." This does not present a peaceful friendship; even if Suzy and her husband were having problems, I am sure she wouldn't want everybody knowing about it. We, as moms and wives, can be very protective of our families. One can totally obliterate her integrity by opening her mouth. I heard it once said that it was better to be thought a fool than to open your mouth and remove all doubt.

Someone who knows Gwen asked me once what Gwen thought about a certain situation. I got really close to her and whispered in her ear, "I'm not going to tell you." I wasn't being rude, I was just protecting my friend.

We don't drag each other down to others, and we don't do it to each other.

When you learn of subjects that are sensitive to your friend, don't even mention them. If she brings it up try not to say much then.

I am hard on myself about some things which Gwen is aware of, but she does not criticize me. I have gained weight lately, and never once have I heard any comments about it. Sometimes the truth is worth keeping to yourself. The truth not only hurts but it can be damaging and, many times, unnecessary to mention.

So, be very careful about how you relate to your friend's husband. He can make or break your friendship. If the husband gives up and allows the friendship in spite of a lot of adversity, or the marriage ends because of your friendship, even in part, God will not bless the friendship and it may end up dead.

It is so important to facilitate peace in their family. Don't put stress on your friend by sandwiching her between you and her husband. It has been my experience that when I am with the whole family, I need to be friends with them all. Do not separate yourself with your friend in the company of others. One way *not* to get invited to functions with their family is to try and isolate yourself with your friend. This is inappropriate codependent behavior.

Try to include everyone in all conversations.

Participate in the activities at hand and don't sit alone. You might be perceived as antisocial.

Men have an innate sense of competition. They compete as children, and grow up to play sports, to achieve, and to win promotions. They even compete with their siblings. When a man comes home, he wants to relax and enjoy his family. At least that is the way it should be.

When men marry, they should naturally want to protect their wives and children as I have said. Our society has turned itself upside down by listening to women's rights activists who are seeking to compete with men and are making an all-out effort to suppress the appropriate role God has created for men. So when they come home they are seeking refuge, comfort, and release from competition.

I decided early that I was not going to compete with Gwen's husband. Competing for the attention of anyone is inappropriate, and for a woman to compete with the husband for the attention of his wife is unacceptable, unscriptural, and dangerous.

He has the final authority over his wife and if she is truly striving to be a woman of God, she would have to choose her family over a disruptive friend. Anyone who causes that kind of disruption is no kind of friend. My friend's husband and I don't share a lot of depth, and I was a little concerned about what he would think of this book. All fears and apprehensions were put to rest when I gave him a rough draft of this book, which he read during a beach holiday.

The verdict per Gwen was: "He was favorably impressed."

Gwen, also not sure of what she would think, read the book which, she stated, put her fears to rest because she did not want her personal life spread around.

Chapter Nine
Preparation

Today as I was out shopping, I began to feel a heaviness that I have felt coming on, but had not become totally aware of it until the last week or so. I had felt it in some ways for several months. Today, however, I felt the weight trying to settle in. At one point I wanted to cry while in a restaurant having lunch. I am sure that it was not PMS or menopause because I know God was doing something with me.

Previously, when I would feel something akin to this, it would usually be associated with a perceived rejection or a time in one of my friendships when I felt my friend was trying to turn away from me. The emotion, while similar, is not quite the same.

When I came home I began to feel hungry. In my mind I said, "God, I am hungry, but not for this soup I am eating. I am hungry for you. I feel like a spiritual anorexic, as if I am starving for you. Please, God, help me. I need you. Lord, in the past when I have felt Gwen distancing herself from me, I have felt intensely and lonely, almost like I am feeling now. But Lord, I want to thank you that I don't feel that way anymore. The intensity has left, and while I may feel sad, I don't feel tense and dejected. Thank you so much, God, that I have come through that. Never do I ever want to feel that way again." You know what? I really believe God has done a work in getting that out of me.

As I went to my room and sat on my bed with the lights out and prayed, I still felt heavy. However, I was pouring out my heart to "My Hero," the one who is able to do anything and everything in and through me to heal me, to cleanse me, to lift any yoke off me and to see me through any problem that may find its way to me. He meets all my needs. There is nothing He is not capable of handling.

My friend Gwen is also a hero, someone I admire. After I prayed I called her and told her how I felt. I told her of the heaviness and the emotions of the day. I poured myself out to her as best I could, but she is a person. She is unable to look into my heart and see the hurt, hear my heart's cry, or see the little girl that was crying out to God. Only God could know those things, but

He is so good and so faithful that He gave me the privilege of a friend who is willing to listen and give advice that comes from her heart and is usually put there by God Himself. That is one reason I see her as a hero; she is full of the Spirit of God. Still, He is my ultimate need-supplier. He is my counselor, my stabilizer, my rock, my salvation. Not Gwen.

Friends cannot meet all our needs. Sometimes He uses our friends, but not always. How He chooses to meet those needs not met by spouses, children, friends, pastors, or whoever is solely His decision. It is *not* the problem of other people, it is God's problem, and He has a whole universe of resources which humans do not have.

It is all right to have needs that are not met by people, because when God meets them it is such a treat to have them finally met. He does such a good job. All the waiting we did to get to that place was only preparation to be able to receive it. That makes the waiting worthwhile and the receiving of it so much more joyful.

When you were a child and you asked your dad for a bicycle, but he did not give it to you right away, he must have had a reason. Perhaps your legs were not long enough. Had he given you a bike while you were too short you might have gotten frustrated, injured, and disillusioned. You may have come to hate the bike and would possibly never have learned to ride. However, since your parent was wise and waited until you could enjoy it, you were able to learn and do well. Granted, you may have fallen and gotten hurt, but you could get up and start again.

I was not ready for a close friend at age ten. My preparation lasted until I was almost forty-one years old. Had God given me Gwen any time sooner, I probably would have blown another friendship. Since I waited, God met my needs all those years and He did it in the ways He chose, not in the ways I expected. He used a lot of people, not just a few. My needs were met in ways that were truly wonderful. Sometimes I did not like the experiences as I went through them, but the result was always beautiful.

When the time came for Gwen and me to meet and become friends, I could not have picked any better scenario or any better circumstances. The joy I have experienced from this friendship is indescribable. Truly, it was well worth the wait. Should God do as I feel He has promised and bring me a husband, it will have been worth the wait as well. Plus, God fulfilled almost all my requests that I had made for a friend. If He does that with a husband, I am in for some great times and a beautiful relationship.

God is never slack about His promises, and He is never late. I wish He would come a little early but He is never early either.

Chapter Ten
Being in Agreement

"Again, I tell you that if two of you on earth agree about anything you ask for, it will be done for you by my Father in Heaven. For where two or three come together in My Name, there I am with them." Matthew 18:19-20.

Gwen and I have committed our conversations to God. He is always invited to sit with us. Without Him we would not be able to enjoy the blessings He has given us. The foundation of all relationships should be Jesus, and we committed our friendship to Him when we realized that He was guiding us into this relationship.

One of the things we talk about when we get together is how things are going with our friends. Sometimes something in the newspaper or on the news will prompt a discussion. We try very hard not to gossip, and usually the subject will be brought up like this: "Gwen, I'd like for you to be in agreement with me that the Joneses will be safe on their trip. That no harm will come to them, no accidents, no illnesses, and may God bless them with a lovely vacation." Or maybe like this: "Did you hear the pastor announce that Mrs. Smith is in the hospital and she has cancer? Let's be in agreement that God will intervene in her life and heal her and that God would give the family peace, strength, and joy in these hard times. Also that God would provide for the hospital bill and for the finances of the family."

Innumerable times we speak in agreement over many things happening to other people, because the Word also says that in what ways we judge and speak about others will be returned to us. Gwen and I decided that we want others to speak well of us and bless us so we make a habit of doing so to and for others.

I love the verse in Ecclesiastes 4:12 which says, "Though one may be overpowered, two can defend themselves, a cord of three strands is not quickly broken." Jesus, Gwen, and I are a threesome and that means we are an unbeatable team. If we remain in agreement within the will of God, who can be against us?

Chapter Eleven
Speaking Blessings

The Word of God tells us to "bless and curse not." I find it a blessing itself that somewhere along the path of our friendship that Gwen and I picked up on the principle that we were to bless others in all that we do and say. Just where it came into being in our lives I cannot say, but it has become literally a part of our commitment to one another.

It is very common for one of us to say to the other when we are getting ready to part or to hang up the phone, "May you be blessed and prosper in all that you do and in your going out and coming in. I have begun to bless people when I leave work: "May you all be blessed" or "Have a blessed evening." I chuckle sometimes to think that in so doing I have influenced another employee to say to me as she leaves, "May you have a peaceful and blessed shift." It has been interesting to note that it makes a difference. One girl would not let me leave unless I blessed her.

Some people will say "Good Luck," but I place no value on luck. Luck is hit and miss, but God pours His blessings continuously and abundantly. I have heard a prominent minister say he researched the word "luck" and found its root in the name Lucifer.

It is also interesting to note that people will respond with a more pleasant "thank you," and even return the blessings. Don't be afraid to receive a blessing. When someone blesses you don't say, "I hope so." Just receive it.

In humorous moments we will get a little carried away and exaggerate the blessings. When one will speak a blessing the other will reply: "May the same blessings fall upon you also." It becomes fun when we can see the joy God brings flow out to the other person. This is part of the foundation of the friendship that is truly Godly, the seeking of the best for the other person.

Personally, the joy I have received from the positive atmosphere in this friendship has been very cleansing to my spirit. The pessimistic aura around previous experiences I have had does not come into play here, because we have committed to making optimism a priority.

When I was a child, someone said something to me on three occasions. Each time the same thing was spoken. Then after I was married my husband made the same statement to me. I will only say it was an undeserved curse.

It is not necessary to say, "I curse you...." All you have to do is make a statement. Have you said or heard someone say to a child: "You are a real dummy. You'll never amount to anything." Then the child begins with, or continues, inappropriate behavior. They don't do well in school, or they end up in trouble. We need to speak positive things to people even if they are doing things inappropriately. Build them up, don't tear them down.

Do you laugh at or tell dumb blond jokes?

Some of my pet peeves are TV programs depicting men as being stupid. One program where everybody is supposed to love the main character portrays this man as being sex-starved and stupid, while his wife enjoys a "normal" personality and outlook. Even commercials have women knowing it all and confident, while the men follow behind groveling and sniveling. The men are being cursed by our own depiction of them as being subnormal.

James talks about the tongue being able to do some real damage, and in one of John's letters he talks about murdering the character of someone with what you say.

Again I refer you to Matthew 12:35-37 and Proverbs 18:21.

We need to stop cursing others and "confess our sins to one another that we may be healed." Don't forget, there is healing in obedience. It is obedient to watch our tongues.

Chapter Twelve
Spiritual Warfare

"The weapons we fight with are not the weapons of the world. On the contrary, they have divine power to demolish strongholds. We demolish arguments and every pretension that sets itself up against the knowledge of God and we take captive every thought to make it obedient to Christ," 2 Corinthians 10:4-5.

Through Jesus, God has given us the power to stand against the forces of darkness. We call it Spiritual Warfare. This warfare is powerful.

A Christian broadcast did a segment on the churches of New York City and surrounding cities whose members have collectively gathered with other believers to pray for crime in the city to decrease. I have watched the news eagerly to see how this has transpired, and was elated to hear that the crime rate had indeed fallen by several percentage points. The unfortunate thing is that the secular newscasts reporting the reduced rate attributed it to the upscaling of police and educational efforts. It is sad that God is not getting credit for this.

In Gwen's and my friendship, it is common for one of us to tell the other of a situation or read something in the paper and the other will say: "I rebuke that in the Name of Jesus. Stop talking about that. I don't believe that is going to happen."

Many times we have prayed and stood firm in spiritual warfare, trying to hold strong to the fact that we can initiate the power God has given us to make a difference.

Chapter Thirteen
Differences, Freedom, and Other Friends

When I prayed those thirty years for a friend, I desired to share the inner recesses of my soul to someone who wouldn't laugh or think ill of me. I wanted a "soul sister." Sometimes, however, it is not possible to share all. Some of the dearest things to you will not necessarily be received or appreciated by your best friend because that may not be where her interest lies.

For instance, when I travel, I take lots of pictures. When I visited Israel I took twenty-nine rolls of film. The first time in Ukraine I took fifteen rolls. When I went to Moldova I only took nine rolls of film but I also took two and a half hours of video. I want to remember every moment.

I wanted to share with Gwen all the neat experiences I'd had. Every tidbit, every detail. You know what? She is not a great picture lover and I have had to learn that probably she will not see a fraction of my still pictures. They are not a big deal to her. I did however, get her to watch about thirty minutes of edited video.

In any relationship you must consider what is important to the other person and do for her what is important to and for her, even if it means giving up your "rights" or privileges. If you truly love someone you will do anything it takes to make them happy, including forfeiting your own desires simply because it is such a joy to see them happy.

If that sounds like a real drag, just do what the other person wants. Try it on a consistent basis. You will begin to see the other person do for you what you want, and you may not even have to tell them what you want or even ask them to do it. In essence, you are respecting them and yielding to them those things that keep peace in the relationship on a Godly level.

Friendships are not necessarily very different from relationships between husbands and wives, because in a successful marriage the partners must be friends. (Hopefully, best friends.) Many of the considerations are the same, such as respect for the other person's thoughts, concerns, feelings, likes, and dislikes.

I have learned so acutely that my friend is sometimes a loner and doesn't want anyone to enter her personal space. Even if I am in crisis, I must honor her time for herself. This has been difficult, because when I am in crisis I need a special person to unload on. It has been in these times that I have had to go to God and lean on Him and not seek human comfort. That is sometimes very stressful, because God does not always provide immediate feedback.

There were times early in the friendship that I wanted to cling tightly as I had in years past. Somewhere in my heart and soul, however, God told me that if I played the part of an all too eager codependent, I could count on squeezing the life out of this friendship as I had many others. So I determined that I would not do this again and I would learn what it took to stop that behavior.

I remember a poster with a butterfly that read, "If you love something, set it free. If it returns to you, it is yours. If it doesn't, it never was." How true.

God has blessed me with the assurance that I have not squeezed the life out of this friendship. We need to encourage our friends to develop other relationships and friends. I cannot tell you what a boost to your own friendship this will be. It is like setting free the butterfly. If your friend doesn't come back to you, maybe she wasn't your friend in the first place. It gives her the opportunity to prove her part of the friendship. It is also a great indicator of how much she treasures your friendship.

Once a week Gwen and some ladies from our church go golfing. I think this is great for her. She has always wanted to learn to golf. This time gives her the opportunity to learn from others and share with them. As much as I would like to be included in this, I will not invite myself nor will I attempt to become part of that group.

The things Gwen learns from them she brings back to share with me, and it actually enhances the relationship we have.

You have to let go in order to get back.

Chapter Fourteen
Calling It Forth

Gwen and I have a little thing we do when things get lost, or we need something and don't have any money for it. We say, "Call it forth." In other words, "Ask and it will be given to you; seek and you will find; knock and the door will be opened to you." Matthew 7:7. If we can ask and it will be given, asking in faith believing, and then we are also given the power to bind and loose; we have a connection that won't quit.

For instance, my daughter came to me crying. She had lost the sapphire from a ring her dad had given her for Christmas. Apparently, it had been an expensive ring. I told her to call it forth, but her reaction was "Yeah! Right." So I called it forth for her without her knowing it. A few weeks later she came running to me yelling, "Mommy, Mommy, I found it. I found it! I found my sapphire. I saw something funny on the floor and I picked it up." Like the woman who had lost the gold coins in her house and found them, we rejoiced.

I am not suggesting that God is a genie that you can just speak to and He will give you everything you want. God loves us and is concerned about everything in our lives. In the Psalms it says to "Delight yourself in the Lord and He will give you the desires of your heart." Psalm 37:4.

When my daughter's car began to fall apart, in June of 1996, I told God I needed a new car and called one forth. I did not want a used car, because I don't like buying someone's old headache. So one day I went to look for a car but had actually told God that if His will was for me to have a used car I'd take what He gave me.

I went to a used car lot, though I was not really expecting to buy just yet. This particular lot is owned by Christians who make it a priority to be honest in all their dealings.

I looked around, and everything either had too many miles or cost too much. Finally, the salesman said, "I have a little '94 Tracer over here that is brand new but it has a stick-shift." I thought, "I don't like Fords, but I'll look at it."

When I saw it, it had only eighty-six miles on it. He had reduced the price to fifty dollars over cost. It had sat on his lot for four months and no one wanted it. It was brilliant blue and I was attracted to it. I asked, "Why has no one bought it?" He said, "Seems like people nowadays don't like driving a manual shift and don't want to learn." Not a problem for me.

So I drove it to Gwen's. She looked at it and thought it was nice. I said, "What do you think? Should I buy it?" In true form she said, "I won't say one way or another. That's between you and God." A lot of help she was! I wanted her to tell me what I should do.

`It still had two and a half years warranty. I know God led me there to buy this car. I had asked God and called it forth.

Gwen has called forth a new stove and oven, a new kitchen floor, and a new vehicle. Not all at the same time, of course, but it really worked.

One thing to remember is that God does bring things that we need and have called forth, but in His time not ours.

Since the writing of this chapter, I have had to call forth a newer car for my daughter. God provided not only the car but the job to pay for it. This has taught my daughter how to operate in God's realm with the authority He has given us.

God will not give us all we ask for because He knows what is good for us. He knows how to give good gifts to His children, and He will not let us down. His word says He will not withhold any good thing from us.

Calling forth things will not be granted to us as God's children if we have not been faithful to God in our giving to Him and in our attitudes. Our parents probably did not reward us for our bad behavior when growing up. God, who is absolutely just and who disciplines us, will not honor any disobedience.

Deuteronomy 28 is very specific about how God deals with obedience and disobedience. Later, when the children of Israel continued with blatant idolatry, He initiated His Words spoken in Deuteronomy 28:15-68. More were the curses of God than the blessings, indicating to me that God is intent on punishing the infidelity of His people.

Chapter Fifteen
Obedience and Forgiveness

I have mentioned several times that healing comes from obedience. Being obedient can be the hardest thing God asks us to do.

When we were going through our divorce, my husband moved to a spare room down the hall and put a lock on the door. He very diligently remembered to lock that door.

He stated to me that he had "evidence" that he was going to take to court that would cause the authorities to award custody of our daughter to him. My curiosity was stimulated as to what this "evidence" was. (He did not, however, win custody.)

One day he locked his keys in the room and had to break in the door frame, which left the room open when he was gone.

While he was gone, I went into the room and searched the whole room to see if I could find what this evidence was. The only thing I found was some insulting literature and a conviction from God that I needed to confess my sin to my husband that I had snooped.

I was mortified that God would ask me to do such a thing. I was so afraid of what my husband would think that I said to God, "Lord, I can't do that. Please don't ask me to do that. I choose, Lord, to fall into your merciful hands. Do to me as you like, but please, the only thing I ask is that you not take away my friendship with Lisa."

God was merciful, but it was at this time He said not to renew the friendship with Lisa. God had made His decision and it would not be changed. I was devastated.

I cannot say how it would have turned out had I been obedient and confessed my sin of snooping. I can say I probably would have had more peace than I had at that time, simply because I would have been obedient.

There are people in my life that God has said He wanted me to forgive.

How do you forgive someone who has molested your child or has taken immoral advantage of your children? If you really want to get a loving mother really angry, mess with her children. I heard a woman speaker say, "There is no difference between a praying mother and a pit bull except the pit bull doesn't wear lipstick".

When God began to deal with me about forgiving others, there were a whole lot of people I would have to forgive. It has taken a while to get over some very hard things, but I have reached a place where I am now able to look some of them in the eye and say "I forgive you."

Whatever is bound on earth will be bound in Heaven and whatever is loosed on earth will be loosed in Heaven. I think that applies to forgiveness and unforgiveness as well. If you refuse to forgive, unforgiveness is bound to you by your refusal to forgive. That also means that if you release forgiveness onto those you have held unforgiveness to, you will also be released.

Jesus is coming back for a spotless bride. That means she will have no sin. Unforgiveness is sin. It is just possible that those who have unforgiveness may get to stay here and not be raptured out with the Bride of Christ. Not just unforgiveness but bitterness, anger, hostility, and all those negative things that motivate those inner responses to others and our surroundings.

I don't want anything to keep me on this earth when Jesus comes back for His bride.

When Jesus says to forgive, regardless of the offense, you *must* forgive. Forgive that ex husband who cheated on you. You don't have to go back to him, but you do have to forgive him. Those thieves who broke in and stole your household goods or those people who violated your child. We have been commanded to forgive them all.

It was hard because my innermost being said, "I want to kill them for what they did to me or my child," but vengeance is God's to repay. You have no idea of the peace that comes with letting go of that bondage. Because, you see, you are the one in bondage to the unforgiveness not the other parties. Your unforgiveness affects you, not them.

Be obedient!

Chapter Sixteen
Entering Into His Presence

One of the things I really love about Gwen is that she is ready at any time to jump into the presence of God. I am so impressed that with a few words, a strain of music, a concept that is revelatory, or just any inclination that presents itself as pointing to God, she is ready to reach out and grab it.

I enjoy many of the ways God uses her to help me see Him. He leads the two of us into times that usher us into His presence.

One Sunday evening Gwen said to me that she wanted to pray about a certain family and professional situation that included some decisions her husband had to make. We went to a certain place and began to pray. The prayer came in increments, with pauses filled with The Holy Spirit. We ended up on our faces, praising God and not wanting to leave, but not before The Holy Spirit made it known to us that we were in the right place at the right time and doing the right things.

Another time she told me of was when she just wanted to hear the doorbell ring, answer it and have it be Jesus; then just sit at His feet and drink in every word. I can easily picture her as Mary of Bethany, sitting at Jesus' feet.

It seems that these times are effortless for her, but to me it is so difficult to be so spiritually spontaneous.

Ultimately, Jesus is the only way into the presence of God, but He does use others to get us to Himself. I am so thankful Gwen is willing to be used to help others get to God. Her husband is very fortunate to have such a faithful wife, whose heart and mind are on serving God and entering His presence. May I ever be as faithful in my relationship to God and to others.

Chapter Seventeen
Being Willing to Change

Gwen has told me the one thing she is so impressed with is my willingness to change. As I see myself, I am not so willing to change. I don't like the stress, pain, and sometimes loneliness. To me, change hurts and I don't willingly submit myself to walk into painful circumstances.

On the other hand, Gwen wants to change. She doesn't like where she is in certain things, and wants them to change. Therefore, she must change if she wants to see results elsewhere. Not so with me. I don't always see that if I change, something or someone else will also.

In her honesty with me, Gwen has told me that if I am not willing to change and grow into a more Godly person who seeks God, she will "leave me in the dust." I believe it. God is using her as a carrot to bring me along. She is not trying to do the controlling or changing me herself. She is leaving that to me.

Since I have found in this friendship the gift from God I had prayed for, I am not willing to give it up. Giving up would mean not changing (and I *do* like the results, if not the process). It would mean the loss of my friend, and the breakage of that covenant that I made to God and to Gwen, as David and Jonathan did. I have broken promises to God before, and I don't want to go there again.

My motivation for change, in my opinion, is a knowledge that I could lose something very precious if I do not. In my marriage I was not willing to change as I should have. Perhaps if I had been more determined to change into the wife I was supposed to be, my husband might not have left me. I have learned from my mistakes and the mistakes of others. Plus, I asked God once why I was so willing to work so hard for this friendship. He told me that it was the only thing that I had ever felt strongly enough about to change my behavior in order to keep it.

My willingness to change was challenged just a week ago. I had asked God what to give up for Lent. Not all people observe this, but I have felt that God answers our questions even in diverse doctrinal beliefs.

He said that He wanted me to decrease the amount of phone calls I make to Gwen.

She had not said anything to me about it and I did not tell her what I felt God had said to me. Well, this stirred inside me until I could hold it no longer, so when I told Gwen about it, it confirmed some stirrings in her.

As I have mentioned, I am the one who needs contact more than she does. She likes solitude. I don't. When I asked God, "Why do you want to restrict our time?" I was impressed with His answer. He said, "Because I want to spend some time with her."

Now, Gwen has the type of personality that people just love. Everybody wants to bond with her. I feel very blessed that God ordained us to be friends. That means I get to bond with my friend with God's blessing.

I do not feel as though I was an obstacle to God's being able to have her attention. If I had not been willing to finally say to God, "Yes, Lord, whatever you want," then I would have become a barrier. Then I would have had to be humbled or removed.

Obversely, I believe God also wants my attention. He wants *our* fellowship every bit as much as we want our friends' attention because He is our friend. Were it not for Him and His great mercy and abundant gifts, we could not have deep and lasting friendships. We *need* to seek Him first and let Him be the foundation.

If for any reason God separates two people who are Christians, it could be because one continues to grow in Him and the other is dragging her feet.

Should you become "unequally yoked" in the area of growth, one could hold the other back, hindering the growing person's ministry. Then it would be God's prerogative to break up the friendship, whether or not there was a covenant. Since covenants were His idea, He can do what He wants with them.

Chapter Eighteen
Encouragement

Everyone has times when things don't go well or as planned. Times when we just want to play ostrich and stick our head in the sand and let the world go by. We are no different than the rest of the world in this.

Many have been the times when I have called Gwen to cry on her shoulder, and I have been blessed by her gift of encouragement. While she is so wonderfully adept at sympathy, she is also capable of "spanking me in the spirit" when I need it.

When she is in her sympathy mode I will hear things like "All is well," or "It will be fine. Don't worry, just walk in it. God is showing you a new thing." Then, when she is in her spanking mode and not sympathetic, she is kind but firm in saying, "Rose, this is one of those times you need to hang in there and listen to God. If you don't you'll miss something and end up missing a blessing. You can't do this or be this way."

We find it interesting how God will change us or work with us in similar ways at the same time or within the same time frame.

One day as I was visiting Gwen she was painting her kitchen. I said to her that I was glad it was her and not me. Within a month or so God told me to buy a house which I had to paint as soon as I moved in. Thankfully, she graciously came to help me. One of the fun things we have said in times when we have been doing some special project is that we will go visit the other to observe the outcome and say, "It looks clean", emphasizing the word clean by saying "cleen."

Even now as I write this we are having a period of growth where God is weaning both of us from some things that make us comfortable. God is showing us these things in order to remove those crutches that we lean on; He wants us to rely on Him and seek Him for comfort. For each of us, the things we must relinquish give us that "warm fuzzy" we both think we need to get along. Apparently, God thinks we don't need them.

These times have in themselves been an encouragement to know that we are both having similar difficulties. It gives us comfort, and strength to face the struggle that lies ahead, knowing the other one is there and being a cheerleader for us.

It is so important to be able to hold your friend or spouse up when they need you, and I have needed Gwen. Sometimes the most effective thing is the simplest, and I like keeping things simple. The less complicated something is, the better I like it. The most effective thing and the simplest is prayer.

Prayer is not just saying, "Sure I will pray for you", it is actually doing it. I had two former patients say to me within two days of each other (almost verbatim), "You prayed for me. You did not just say that you would pray, but you asked "May I pray for you now'? I really felt much better after you prayed for me."

So it is with us as individuals. We love to have someone pay that little bit of attention to us. Praying is a better way to do it.

Our technique is to lay a hand on the other's forehead and say something like, "Thank you, Jesus, for my friend, and I ask that you would show yourself powerful and heal her. Relieve her of her pain and remove the source. I lose any cancer in the Name of Jesus. And please replace what is left void with Your Spirit. Cover her with the Blood of Jesus. Amen."

There are times when we feel it justified to anoint someone with oil. Though I usually use olive oil, I have used perfumed oil or cooking oil. I know anointing does work. It is scriptural to anoint people. James 5:14-16 says, "Is any one of you sick? He should call the elders of the church to pray over him and anoint him with oil in the Name of The Lord. And the prayer offered in faith will make the sick person well; the Lord will raise him up. If he has sinned he will be forgiven. Therefore confess your sins to each other and pray for each other that you may be healed. The prayer of a righteous man is powerful and effective."

Women must be careful, though. When in a group where a man is presiding, a woman needs to ask or suggest to anoint. If the man in charge say "no", then you must yield to his authority even if you feel God has said to anoint. You are relieved of any responsibility.

God will deal with the person in charge. Never is a woman allowed to usurp the authority of the man God has placed in charge.

When women are meeting and praying, if it seems good to anoint, you must get the permission of the person or persons involved. Some people are not in agreement with anointing and you will only cause division if you force the issue.

While on a mission trip to a former Soviet country I wanted to anoint some children. However, I learned before we asked the pastor that another denomination had forcefully confronted that particular church with certain doctrines, one of which was anointing. Instead of unifying and bringing the Body of Christ together, they ended up permanently divided.

The times of prayer and anointing are meant for the encouragement and edification of the Body of Christ. Using these tools indiscriminately can destroy relationships.

Chapter Nineteen
Honoring God

When my husband and I divorced in 1987, I moved south on the instruction of God. He was very specific about that. Not long after I moved south a prophet of God came to our church and gave this prophecy specifically to me: "Daughter, I am doing a new thing in your life. And yea I brought you among this people and among this community and among this present movement of My Spirit to more instruct you in the more excellent way.

"And, oh, surely you shall be able to glean, and ye shall be able to know, and you will be comfortable with the happenings that shall take place. And don't make thy decisions too quickly. For Oh, it is easy to snap to a decision. But yea, 'Make naught of thy decisions too quickly' saith the Lord, for, daughter, I want to show you this thing from several angles. 'And I want to be able to convince you,' thus saith God, 'What is happening is present to truth.' And yet let not even the word of another confuse you in this that I am doing. But Oh, you are not the garbage can of my purpose and yea I will not allow someone to dump in thy life that that is not of me. And I will keep you and protect you. And I will surely acknowledge unto to you that I am well able to do exceeding abundantly above all that you would ask or think.

"And this is the beginning of new days,
And this is the beginning of new ways.
And this is to position you more acutely to My Will
and this is to help you go up the high and Holy Hill.
And this is to let you even know my voice
and this is to give you the opportunity to make a choice.
And this is to stimulate that faith from within.
And this is to let you know why I saved you from sin.
And this is to cause you to seek my face.
And this is to let you understand that your life's in My hand.
And this is to prepare you even for a day that yet is.
And this is to let you know that you are not your own, you're His.

"Therefore, don't jump too quick and go off the handle,
and yea, pick up thy duds and get in thy sandal.
And Oh, don't even want to go afar
and put the key in the ignition and drive the car.
And Oh, don't even say this, 'I'm through',
and yea walk out the door and thy face looks like you're blue.
For daughter, I'm not through with you yet.
I don't want you to leave and even fret.
I want you to know that I am The King
and I am going to give you a reason to sing."

For some people this type of occurrence is foreign, but I know beyond the shadow of a doubt that God used that man to speak to me. Every thing he said was characteristic of me, and he had never met me.

God was telling me He was watching me closely and was interested in my future. What He was saying was that He knew my temperament and knew that when I got frustrated I could easily get up and move. I was used to mobility and had no problem adjusting to my surroundings.

I have always been quick to make snap decisions, regardless of the consequences, so I would not have to deal with problems. I would even accept less than the best, so I would not be bothered with the burden of making a decision. Since then I have learned to wait and receive a much bigger blessing because I was willing to hold off from making decisions. Had I waited on God's timing and choice of a mate, I probably would have found the right man and still be married, having saved a lot of people a lot of misery.

I really needed that prophecy. It was accurate then and has proven to be accurate since. God has honored me by keeping His promises and has expected me to do the same.

If we honor God, He will honor us. In 1 Samuel 2:1, it says, "My heart rejoices in the Lord; in the Lord my horn is lifted high." In the footnotes it reads: "To have one's horn lifted up by God is to be delivered from disgrace to a position of honor and strength." That is what I want! To be honored by God and blessed by Him.

God had moved me to prepare me. I specifically asked God why He moved me to Georgia and His answer pleased me: "To teach you how to be a friend." I learned a lot about that from so many precious people in Georgia.

When I finally realized my husband was serious about the divorce, I said to God, "I am sorry, Lord, for not fulfilling my promise to be a missionary. Please forgive me, and I will go where you will send me." I soon read Steve Lightle's book *ExodusII* which tells of preparations for the return of the Jews to Israel from Europe. I said, "God, this is where I want to go." Then He answered..., "That is where I am calling you to go."

I was late in honoring God with my promise, but it is better to be late than never to honor your word. Oddly, I have kept my word to humans better than I have to God. He should be the one I should have striven to honor most. I have tried to correct that problem.

Honoring God is not just doing mission work. It is doing His will right where we are now.

Perhaps the highest priority on my list is my chastity. In the years since our divorce I have dated four men. All of them professed themselves to be Christians; one of them worked in a Christian organization. All of them wanted to have sex with me. The last one was the most polite, he asked me if I would have sex with him, instead of expecting to just be able to take it. I politely declined and took it as an opportunity to share with him what God's Word says about unmarried sex.

When I married the man I spent sixteen years with, I was a virgin. We fought the temptation to have premarital sex, and won. Of all the things I treasure about my marriage, I cherish my chastity most. When the divorce was final, I "set my face like flint"; I decided that I would again retain my chastity and obey God's Word. My bed would not be defiled, and since the last time I arose from my husband's bed, I have kept myself pure. This is only one way of honoring God.

It is imperative to abstain from illicit sexual relations. To resist Satan's temptations should be your ultimate desire for purity. I am convinced there would be less divorce, fewer unwed mothers, and a decline in shattered lives if people would just practice abstinence until marriage.

There is more to sex than just the act of two people joining their bodies together. In the spiritual realm of Spiritual Warfare, there is a uniting of the unseen between two people. If they are not married, there is an unnatural attachment that develops. This causes conflict between the powers of light and darkness. The result is not the romantic thrill that Hollywood would have us believe.

The outcome is usually infidelity. There is a lack of commitment between two partners who have no sense of what it means to hold fast to moral values. The powers of light have no strength, because God's Word has not been set in motion.

Much of this generation has grown up on river banks, in boats on the lake, at the beach, or on hiking trails on Sunday mornings. The Bible has been left out of the curriculum and the parents have provided this example.

After my daughter broke up with a boyfriend she had dated for one and a half years, she told me that she and he were still friends although she is now married to someone else. My response to her was, "You could not have remained friends if you had had sex with him." It is so very hard to face someone you have been intimate with.

The television and newspapers are filled with tragic stories of stalkers harassing and even murdering their partners. Many times they have been to bed together. It seems so much harder to release a relationship if those involved have been intimate with one another.

I once attended a wedding of an older couple whose adult children were present. I noticed that the son of one of the wedding participants had his girlfriend with him. As I watched them relate to one another and observed their touch and behavior toward one another, I came to the conclusion that they apparently had been cohabiting with one another. In a conversation I overheard later, my suspicions were confirmed.

It seems the feeling of ownership develops once the union has been made, causing the persons involved to feel a lack of control which can lead to violent behavior. I heard it once said that, "To a guy sex means ownership. To a girl it means commitment." The guy is not interested in commitment and the girl doesn't want to be owned.

When someone enters a homosexual relationship, they have not honored God. The Old Testament Law specifically calls for stoning of homosexuals (Leviticus 20:13). The New Testament condemns it. Romans 1:27 speaks of men receiving the "due penalty for their perversion." I am convinced one of the modern day penalties is AIDS, not to mention the other sexually transmitted diseases. Please understand that I am not against the persons themselves who are gay or lesbian. I am against the sin they commit. This does not honor God.

Over my years of employment, including my years in the military, I have worked with people who were gay or lesbian and I find them to be likable, intelligent, very professional, and committed to their professions. God made it clear to me that I am not to mistreat any of His creation or treat them with contempt, whether or not they are Christians. That was one time God Himself spoke audibly to me and pointed His finger at me. I saw a vision of Him as He said it. My response was a very humble, "Yes, Sir."

Honoring God also means telling the truth. In *Codependent No More*, Melody Beattie says, "Nothing will help us feel crazy faster than being lied to." If that makes *us* feel out of control, it does so to others and causes all kinds of confusion. Being truthful and honorable in every aspect of our lives gives credibility to our witness and speaks volumes about how God is able to work with us.

This won't be easy, because people are afraid of the truth. When trying to sell a car I would tell the people who asked if there were any problems with the car that I had fixed; although the car was in wonderful operating order, it scared them. Nothing was wrong except that I had told them the truth.

When Satan lies and deceives us, we come to a place where we feel crazy. It is then that we usually seek God and confess our sin.

So, honoring God is an achievable goal. If we fail, He forgives us and helps us back in line but we need to consciously seek Him out. We cannot do it alone.

Only in the intimacy of the marital relationship is sex scripturally allowed. I strongly feel the term "making love" is a misnomer. Only God can 'make' love in any of its forms. Anything short of that is a perverted substitute perpetrated by Satan himself.

Since our divorce, I have come to feel that sexual intimacy in marriage should be an expression of joy. It should be a oneness only God can join, and the uniting of two people to make one flesh. This union of one flesh should be an explosion of our exhilaration with our spouse, but in our society it has been reduced to an animalistic act with jokes and insensitivity woven into its very existence.

Granted, each occurrence would not always be the wonderful "explosion" I just mentioned but it should always be a satisfying release of our innermost feelings of love to the other person. It should leave them with a sense of satisfaction and acceptance rarely seen in marriages today. It should not be experienced in premarital or extramarital liaisons.

If God sends me a husband, I pray with all my heart that we both realize the expression of joy and devotion that God alone can give.

There are many other ways to honor God, such as tithing, volunteering for church activities, running errands, and meals on wheels to name a few. Since this is a relationship-oriented book I have made my emphasis just that.

In relationships, honor God with faithfulness, trustworthiness, gentleness, kindness, peacefulness, commitment, love, service to your spouse & friends, and obedience. It is so important to base all relationships on Jesus Christ, because all who know us see how we live and base their opinions on our lives.

Chapter Twenty
The Protection Covenant

Gwen said to me recently that some day I might decide that she was crazy and that I would just decide to be "outta here."

Well, there have been times when I just wanted to walk away and forget the whole friendship. I have not told her of some of the times I have been very disappointed in her. There are times I have felt she was ashamed of me and did not want me around, and at times I feel she is insensitive and thoughtless. These are the times I want to say to her that I am not willing to put up with the attitude that she is always right.

We have our sessions of tears. I have had my times of nearly yelling at her, but I always managed to get my point across without any type of verbal or physical violence. That is from God, because as a child I was ready to fight anyone who crossed me.

On the other hand, I have been known to generate some anger in her, but she is much kinder at delivering her message. Sometimes she just stuffs it and doesn't say anything. Must be that Southern Belle I mentioned previously that is tempered by the Holy Spirit.

The only thing that has kept me from saying to her that "I'm finished", and breaking our covenant, is the fact that I made a promise. I took an oath to be her friend and to be honest to her. Some people really feel that since it is 'only' a friendship, that it would be all right to dump her but God takes no delight in fools who protest to the temple messenger and say "I made a mistake." See Numbers 30:2 and Ecclesiastes 5:4-7.

Also, I found two more references to oaths during the editing of this book. They are applicable in the context of this chapter.

Leviticus 5:4 says, "Or if a person thoughtlessly takes an oath to do anything, whether good or evil—in any matter one might carelessly swear about—even though he is unaware of it, in any case when he learns of it he will be guilty."

Deuteronomy 23:21-23 says, "If you make a vow to the Lord your God, do not be slow to pay it, for the Lord your God will certainly demand it of you and you will be guilty of sin. But if you refrain from making a vow, you will not be guilty. Whatever your lips utter you must be sure to do, because you made your vow freely to the Lord your God with your own mouth."

If God had said to the children of Israel, "I am sending you into exile, and you have only one chance to get it right," He would not be merciful; He would have had to break the covenant when the Israelites messed up. He didn't just dump them when the going got rough. If we are to act like Him and be like Him, then when we make a covenant we are to keep it. There is a need for faithfulness in friendships, too!

If you are one who has trouble keeping promises, then you probably should not make covenants. Marriage could be a hardship for you and you may not be able to sustain a committed friendship.

There is a type of "divorce" that takes place when you walk away from a friendship you have nurtured. A bond has been made; any time a bond is broken there is a tearing away, and a painful process will follow.

So, in my hurt and anger, I have to walk through it, and process it, because if I walk away from that relationship I not only hurt her, I hurt myself. I tear away that part of me that I have shared, that part of my spirit that bonded. I have been torn over friendships before. They were painful, even though I had not made a covenant with them.

I heard a lady speak once whose child asked her a "What if" question. "Mommy, what if one of us dies in an accident or gets hurt?"

She was concerned that Satan might try to destroy someone in her family, so she began to seek God about what to do. After getting an answer, she sat down with her family and made a covenant with all of them. They made an agreement that not one of them would get killed or be taken out by tragedy before it was their time to go. They all prayed together to stand for the protection of their family with God's help, and the way they were going to do it was to plead the Blood of Jesus, listen to the Holy Spirit, and be sober and vigilant.

Here are some of the scriptures she gave as a basis for her motivation: Luke 10:19, 1 Peter 5:8, 1 Thessalonians 5:8-9, Habakkuk 2:1, Romans 10:8-10, Psalm 141:3, 2 Chronicles 16:9a, Isaiah 54:13-16, Psalm 91, John 10:10, Psalm 107:20, and Ephesians 6:10-18.

Once they made the covenant they sealed it with communion.

Later their daughter became gravely ill, so they initiated the covenant they had made. They began pleading the Blood of Jesus and speaking the words of their covenant. They took communion, they asked people to pray, and while the child was not responding they had someone reading scripture to her at all times. Miraculously, the child had a complete recovery with no residual effects.

As I listened to her speak, I felt I needed that kind of coverage for my family. The only person I felt I could turn to was Gwen, who understood the concept of covenants.

When I spoke with her again I told her of the teaching. I felt that we needed to do it over our own families, and she quickly agreed.

We had not actually planned a time to do this, so I was surprised when she called and said that her family had gone to a football game and she was coming over to make our covenant.

I was playing couch potato, so I got up and said, "Okay, God, what shall I do first to prepare for this?" The following thirty minutes were so orchestrated by God that I was awed at how it turned out.

He started me out by washing three small gold tone glasses I had purchased in Moldova. They were communion size. He then had me clean a silver Elijah's cup I had bought in a synagogue. He was very clear that I was to dry them with a freshly washed hand towel. Then He led me to get down my prayer rug I had purchased in Israel and to place a small table in the center of the rug.

This table was to be set with my finest damask. I covered the table, got my Ukrainian serving tray, covered it with a cloth napkin and then set the glasses on the tray in the center of the table. Then I put the Elijah's cup in the center of the three small glasses. I did all He told me. Then He said, "You need a prayer shawl." I knew I did not have a Jewish one, so He told me to get the buffet cloth I had purchased on the street in Kiev, Ukraine. It is a long, hand-embroidered cloth that nicely served the purpose.

Gwen brought the grape juice and anointed the bottle with oil, and we anointed each other. We poured the juice into the Elijah's cup and served it to the three smaller cups. We invited God to partake with us.

We sat down, placed the ends of the shawl each over our shoulders. I began by reading all the scriptures listed, then we listened to Hosanna's *Come To The Table*.

Before taking communion we spoke to each other, promising to pray for each others' families, property, and animals. We also pledged to support one another, and believe in one another. We prayed for excellent health and long life; reaffirmed our honesty and friendship. The whole thing lasted well over an hour. When we finished praying and pledging we took communion.

I have had problems dealing with the fact that I have a friend who loves me so much that she is willing to put that kind of trust in me. She trusted me so much that she would make a covenant with me and place the protection of her family in the hands of God via my prayers. I know that God loves me and sees me as His child and one whom He trusts. That doesn't amaze me because He is God and is He faithful. After so many years of people turning on me, I just felt so confident that no person would ever think enough of me to entrust such a precious thing to me. Well, God was there in our covenant and what a blessing God is.

The very next day I had the opportunity to put that pledge to work. I had received some devastating news. It was a situation that I had prayed to God to intervene and work it out the way I wanted, but He did not work it out the way I had prayed. For about three days I went around in a fog. During that time I asked God a lot of questions.

The news I got caused me to respond in a way that put Gwen ill at ease, thinking I had not trusted God to protect my family. This made her very upset with me, so one of my questions to God was: "What if I were to bail out of this friendship now? Why doesn't Gwen understand my feelings?" Well, He gave me a clear and enlightening answer.

I saw an umbrella with Gwen and me standing under it. The umbrella was the covenant we had made a few days before. God showed me that before we made the covenant I was the person praying alone for protection over my family, and the umbrella I carried before making our covenant was only *my* prayers. When Gwen and I prayed and pledged the covenant, we stood together holding the umbrella. By joining our prayers together, we strengthened the protection. Now, if I were to succeed in giving up on the covenant, I would be tearing a big hole in the umbrella. In essence, I would be breaking the bond with my friend, tearing a hole in the covenant, and leaving those we had prayed for unprotected. After seeing that, I could not go through with any type of "bail out." I am too committed to this friendship to just walk away from it.

At this point I wish to emphasize the depth of seriousness in making a covenant. People get married and divorced as if they were changing clothes. They even enter lightly into relationships that should last forever. When one gets slightly miffed at the other they are ready to walk out because they haven't got what they wanted. That is not love, that is lust and selfishness.

In my friendship with Gwen, I do get annoyed. She has no idea how often because I don't want to hurt her. Being brutally honest is not healthy. I love my friend dearly, and I want to protect her from my negative feelings and emotions because they can be selfish and ruthless. I am sure that if I did not allow God to love her through me, she would not want to be my friend. She would not be able to tolerate the ugliness emanating from me.

Making a covenant can have extremely painful results and can leave someone spiritually dead if the covenant is not kept. That is why it takes God to keep people solid in relationships. *Please!* Don't make even small promises too quickly. Breaking them hurts everyone involved.

When my children were growing up they would ask me for things. I knew that there might be times I would not be able to keep my word, so when they would approach me I would say, "We will see. I make no promises." That way I would not be the big meanie if I was unable to keep my word.

In my vision of the umbrella, I saw a second umbrella with Gwen and her husband holding the umbrella over their family. God showed me that she needs the agreement and covenant of her husband with her in order to finalize and solidify the protection of their family. Her husband is her "Covenant Partner" and she needs to unify with him in all areas of their marriage.

The terminology is important here. Two people who are married are covenant partners. In God's view that's the way it is. While I have partnered in covenants with my friend and that is certainly very binding, there is no bond like the covenant partner bond between a married couple.

When two people who are friends make covenants, they are not covenant partners. I am convinced God's plan is for married people to be "Covenant Partners." This is why homosexual "partners" can never be covenant partners because they, in God's eyes, can never be married.

When a man and a woman come together in marriage, they make a covenant to "...honor, cherish...till death us do part...." This marital covenant is ordained by God. When two people of the same sex come together and want to get "married," scripturally speaking, this is not possible. This is a very foolish thing to attempt and God does not honor it. Again, His Word says He takes no delight in fools.

Chapter Twenty-one
Reconciliation

Today is Easter Sunday, 1998. The sun is shining and there is new life everywhere. Spring has sprung; the azaleas are just beautiful. I love Gwen's driveway which is thickly lined with large Tabor azaleas.

Easter. Nearly two thousand years ago God reconciled the fallen sin-filled world to Himself through the Blood of His only Son, Jesus Christ. He is the God of mercy, forgiveness, and draws the souls of men unto Himself.

Reconciliation. Webster defines it as "...the renewal of friendship between parties at variance. The act or process of harmonizing or making consistent...things apparently opposed..." We are opposed to God in our rebellion and disobedience, but He has provided eternal reconciliation through His Son.

If the God of the universe has all authority and the absolute right to deny forgiveness, if warranted, and doesn't, who are we to withhold forgiveness to others?

I had the great privilege and blessing of reconciling with someone after four years of silence. This person was someone I had offended and realized it after it was too late.

In the interim, I prayed to God many times to heal that relationship I so desperately missed. I never heard from my friend. One night after work, I came home to hear her voice on my answering machine. I was elated, but it was too late to call her back, so I had to wait until the next day.

Uncertain of what to expect, I did have great joy and peace that held me through the night. This told me I had nothing to worry about.

When we spoke the next day, I felt that our hearts had reconnected in a way like never before. I felt a bonding with her that I had never felt before. She had forgiven me.

We laughed and shared about our children and my grandchild-to-be. I told her about my book; then I realized the book would not be finished unless I wrote on reconciliation.

There is joy in reconciling that cannot be found elsewhere. To be able to know forgiveness and return into the heart of the other person is so exhilarating. When it is ordained by God there is little to compare to it.

How deeply touched I was to hear from her. I won't see her for a while because she lives far away, but I can't wait to wrap my arms around her. The delight and happiness that has come back to me is an answer to prayer, and an indication that God loves to see His children happy. I know He is also rejoicing that we have reconnected that severed friendship.

In my friendship with Gwen, since we are so close, she and I have many opportunities to become offended. One of the things we will say when one touches a nerve is that "I am not going to take offense. I am going to leave that 'fence' right where it is." When one takes offense she builds fences and walls that drive wedges between the parties. We decided long ago that we would not take offense, regardless of how painful the situation. Granted, I have nearly taken offense with her, but I have weighed the outcome and prefer the blessing of our friendship over the grudges I would be carrying.

Gwen said recently that "I have committed to not taking offense in our friendship and I will stick to it." She proceeded to tell me kindly how she felt and what she wanted me to do about it.

With my friend with whom I reconciled, it was I who built the walls by what I said. I am willing to carry the burden; because I have been forgiven, there are no walls, no barriers.

Reconciliation is fun once you get past the pride that keeps you from apologizing. Is it worth lying next to your husband back to back, seething over who squeezed the toothpaste in the middle, or even about that huge dent in the car?

To my then husband's credit he said, "It is done and over," when I told him I had sideswiped another car with our brand new Ford Econoline van. There is no point and no ground to be gained from letting the sun go down on your anger. Ephesians 4:26b says "Do not let the sun go down while you are still angry, and do not give the devil a foothold."

Many people view asking forgiveness and forgiving as a sign of weakness. What a deception! It has been rather effective for Satan.

Forgive, and ask for forgiveness. You will find favor with everyone you meet, even when the situation does not call for forgiving someone. Your attitude will reflect this gracious behavior.

Chapter Twenty-two
Relieving the Pressure and Release

In the past couple of years Gwen has been undergoing a change. She knew God was doing something with her, but she wasn't sure what. Because she is one who keeps things inside, she didn't say much to me about it. Many times this year I was left with my own thoughts on why she seemed so distant since I didn't know what was happening with her.

Many of us tend to make our own assumptions of what we think is happening, and we think we know what the other person is feeling or thinking. This was true with me during this time of her change. I thought at times I had a handle on what was going on, and nearly gave up on Gwen. It seemed just too painful.

As I have said previously, when I prayed for so many years for that one special friend, I asked God for a listener who would be a sounding board who would always be there. Of all the people I have ever unloaded on, Gwen has been the best. The absolute, A number one, best listener ever. That is, outside of God. He not only listens, He's got the inside scoop on what is happening all around and within us. Too many times He does only that, just listens. He does not always acknowledge He heard us or let us feel good about His hearing us.

This past year, after experiencing some type of intense situation, I would go to Gwen as always and share the whole story with her at which time I would feel much better. While she would interact somewhat, I noticed a distancing that would concern me. This distance also seemed to permeate many other aspects of our friendship. I was getting pretty wound up about it.

Then Gwen dropped the bomb. "Rose, I can't handle your problems anymore. They are too heavy for me." I was devastated.

I cried out to God, "This was one of the biggest requests on my list of things a friend should be. What is happening here?"

In the process of all this, God gave me an idea for an invention which I am now near to marketing. One Sunday in church I heard Him say, "How bad do you want the invention and the mission work I have called you to? Do you want them bad enough to give up time with Gwen?"

Many times He will ask us to give up something special in our lives in order to bring about something else. He wanted me to lighten up on Gwen and to seek Him instead.

Over the past few months, Gwen and I both felt God was doing something. I didn't have a clue that He was weeding out my need to purge myself of all the pain and hurt by talking about it.

I have been feeling a lot of pressure lately both in our friendship and at work as well. Much of the pressure at work has been from things I have no control over.

When I realized God was asking me to be willing to give up something that was so precious to me I was shocked. My soul was in agony. This was my pressure release system; and He was asking me to give up one of the more wonderful things about my friendship with Gwen. What was He thinking?

Part of what He was thinking was that too many times we talk way too much, and we get ourselves into a truckload of trouble by opening our mouths. He certainly knows how bad I am at that. I spoke in another chapter about our tongues. I feel that in the big scheme of things He was not saying that it was just unloading on Gwen that was my problem. It was *my* inability to control my emotions and to keep things to myself that could be potentially harmful to me and to others.

For instance, when I am released from my current occupation to head for the mission field, I will be headed for some very sensitive areas of the world. I am sure there will be times when I will be frustrated, under pressure, and maybe angry. If I seek out someone to unload on, who will it be? Even if it is another American or another missionary, can I be sure they are trustworthy? God is trying to protect me and is training me well ahead of time. I first realized this and shared with Gwen what I thought to be something sacrificial regarding our friendship, and I was surprised to hear her say that something similar was working inside her. It was a confirmation of what I was hearing from God. She was getting a similar message; what I was saying was meeting a part of her spirit that God was dealing with. This was both a comfort and a concern.

God is cleaning out and bringing to the surface those things that need to be eradicated in order to take us to the next level. I am looking forward to my mission work. I am willing for Him to do what He needs to to clean out my garbage, even if I have to sacrifice some aspect of my friendship.

This friendship is a gift from God. I have no fear of anything being taken from us that is helpful to us. He only wants to make it stronger. I believe strongly that God will not make us break the covenant of friendship that we have made.

In discussing this situation with Gwen, we came to the conclusion that we needed to release one another from the expectation of each other being there for the purpose of being a sounding board. We are still there for each other; we have just released one another from the expectation. There is an added freedom to this release.

If we continue to expect a person to do what we are supposed to give up, then we are keeping a firm grasp on what we have been asked by God to let Him have. This is not good. I can guarantee you that if you are not willing to give up what He wants, you will at some point lose it anyway. We *must obey* God if we want His blessings, and I want His blessings and I want His blessings on my friendship to continue.

One of the things I am very well aware of is that I can lose anything that God has given me if I clutch it too tightly. I will squeeze the life out of it. And as I have mentioned before, if you will let go and give the friendship its freedom, it will flourish.

It is very clear to me that in addition to the other reasons for God to ask this of me, I might have killed a big part of our friendship by continuing to unload on Gwen. If she is unable to handle the pressure, I can kill our friendship with the pressure.

Now, when I was alone with God and He was allowing the reality of this to settle in, I cried. I was hurting. Having to give this to Him hurt a lot, so I said to Him, "God, in the past you have been there to listen to me but you have not always let me know your comfort. You have been silent more than you have spoken. I will need your interaction more and will need for you to comfort me and let me know you have heard. Please give me that presence that has helped me in the past when I have spoken to a friend and felt as though I have been heard."

I have to trust He is going to do that for me since it is a big thing for Him to have asked me to give up something that was very special.

Chapter Twenty-three
Learning New and Sometimes Hard Lessons

When I obtained the copyright for this book, I thought it was a finished product. I have been trying to get it published since then and have hit some brick walls. Several people have said, "Maybe it is not finished yet." I had thought to myself, "What's not finished? If I get no more revelation or inspiration, it must be finished." So I have waited and have begun to pray that God would show me what to do to facilitate the publication of this book. It is not finished, and I am adding to it several years after what I thought was its completion.

In reading this book, you have learned of my life without, and then with a friend that God had provided. There is a phrase I have heard many times in describing what the ultimate ecstasy is, and I think it would describe well my first ten years of this friendship. "I thought I had died and gone to Heaven", because our friendship had grown and become so rooted in God.

When ministers want to describe what God says or feels about us, they will give examples like "If God had your picture He would put it on His refrigerator or carry it in His wallet" or "If God had a bumper sticker your name would be on it." He feels for us like a proud father does. "Proud parent of a terrific kid" kind of pride.

Being single, I am alone a lot. When I need to talk I have been able to call Gwen and usually have been able to unload. In the last one and a half years, however, Gwen has been taking correspondence classes and has had to make trips to the institution to fulfill her requirements.

Most of the time I feel abandoned on these occasions. There are very few Level five (on a scale from one to five, with five being the highest) spiritual people that I am able to communicate with. When Gwen is gone, I feel so alone. I still pray, but as I have mentioned before, sometimes God does not answer me and I feel isolated.

Well, on one of these occasions God spoke to me, but what He said was really far from what I was expecting. Gwen had to take a trip alone, as her husband had already taken his course on that subject.

We all feel sorry for ourselves at some point. This particular time I was having a pity party, wanting Him to sympathize with me, but He was not willing to do that. He said to me, "This is my time with Gwen. I have to get her away from every one who wants her attention so I can have her for me." On a number of occasions since then He has reinforced that thought to me.

Not long after that Gwen told me that she had learned that one of the names of God is Jealous. That never occurred as a name, only as a characteristic. God is jealous over all His children. We are all so important to Him that He will do what it takes to get our attention. I know without a shadow of a doubt that Gwen has a very prominent place in God's heart, because He has separated her on occasion just so He can have her to Himself. He is like that with all of us, and He moves a lot of people just so He can get His way.

Over the last ten years, I have enjoyed great blessings in this relationship. God has been in it and has allowed us to do a lot of things together. Recently that began to change.

I have felt for a number of years that God was initiating a weaning to prepare me for a time when one of us may be separated from the other. When I first realized it, I did not like it. I had arrived to a place in life where I thought "I had died and gone to Heaven."

Sooner or later God will begin to change things, and if you have taken things for granted you can hurt a great deal. Don't let yourself get that comfortable. Certain things about relationships last a short while, and when the changes come it will hurt a lot.

Recently, a situation arose where I was deeply hurt. Something inside me died. In having to walk through this difficult time I have again been faced with the covenants Gwen and I have made. When all the pain comes, and the desire to run resurfaces, I am reminded of the commitments I have made and I have to remain firm in my promises. I seek extra guidance to know what my position is. So far, mostly what I am hearing lately is "Don't do anything, just stand."

Gwen keeps saying that this is of God, but I wonder how such pain can be of God?

Jehovah God is a man of timing and gentleness. I had prayed years ago that if something like this were to happen, He would let me down easy. As difficult as this is, and has been, He has been preparing me to let me down easy.

Our friendship is not over. This is a gift from God. He has promised me that it is not over as far as He is concerned, but my responses are what will further or end this friendship. I can have my way, or I can have the friendship. In fact, I heard a statement on the radio recently that says it most accurately, "If I insist on having this friendship my way, I will lose it forever." Boy, what a ton of bricks!

Just a few days ago while God was revealing more things to me, He showed me something else. Don't ever ask Him to reveal things to you that you may not want to hear, He just might tell you.

While pondering all the hurt and the events that I have touched on, I began to see more clearly why much of this has happened.

In the first ten years of our friendship, many of my needs were being met. While many of Gwen's needs were being met, I was the recipient of the greatest portion of fulfillment. Then He said, "It isn't about you anymore, Rose. It is Gwen's turn to have her needs met." The time has come when those needs of Gwen's that have laid dormant all these years are beginning to surface.

All those years I was not intentionally seeking this, nor was I consciously aware that this was the case. Really, it is quite embarrassing and shameful that I was so thoughtless and careless as not to know that.

So, I have become aware that I need to be more aware of Gwen's needs. It is hard not to call her when I need to talk. It is even harder not to try and place blame on who I see as the source of the restriction, when I simply need to respond and say, "Yes Lord. Whatever you say. I will do it."

This has been a hard chapter for me. I thought some of the earlier chapters were hard, but this one is tough. It exposes me in places I would prefer not to be seen. However, this whole book is about revelation and exposing those things that many people keep inside. They are afraid of what others will think.

Gwen is desirous of maintaining our friendship and is aware that the wrong responses will tear it apart. My desire is to help others know that someone else has paved the way to letting things out, so they can be set free from all that pain. What seems like a lot of pain now is nothing compared to the amount of pain to be experienced if things are left to come out later. Coming clean is never easy, but the longer it is contained, the harder it is to let go. Getting it out removes any opportunity for the devil to live in that pain and taunt you.

It gives you the ability to "take the bullets out of his gun," as Gwen says. He can't shoot you with it anymore.

Loss of a friendship or something precious can be avoided by willingness to say yes to God and endure the temporary pain. It is always best to accept the pain early.

My daughter asked my oldest granddaughter where the toothpaste was after discovering toothpaste smeared on her dresser. She replied, "I don't know, Mommy." My daughter said, "Did you hide it in your bed?" "No, Mommy." "Are you telling me the truth?" "Yes, Mommy. The toothpaste is not in my bed."

Well, that night my daughter went to tuck her into bed, and when she pulled the covers back she found the dilapidated tube of toothpaste. My granddaughter rolled her eyes up to the ceiling and said, "I shouldn't have done that!"

We are like that. We need to open up and purge ourselves of those things that bind us. If we don't, something happens to expose us in a time that may be too late for us to change or for us to change our circumstances. Now is the time to be obedient.

Chapter Twenty-four
How to Talk to Your Friend If There Is a Problem

When Gwen and I agreed to be honest about our relationship, that included every aspect of it. We knew that there would be hard times when we would be afraid to say something because we would not be sure how the other person would accept the information. Nonetheless, it was an agreement that we made and we have stuck to it.

Many of the times I have wanted to dump the relationship and go on my way were right after she had confronted me with something I did not want to hear, usually about how I was imposing on her time, or how her husband had asked her to tell me about something he felt was important.

In relationships, the main cost of maintenance is time. If we have no time to spend with that person the relationship will die. There is nowhere to go with it. Time was what I was requiring of Gwen.

When a person with whom you have a relationship begins to expect a lot of time, it puts a strain on the relationship not to mention the fact the family of the married person may suffer.

I am ashamed to admit it, but I have done this. Many years before I knew Gwen, when I was seeking that friendship and when I was married, I would reach out to people. In reaching out I knew that I was absorbing a lot of their time but I was not always able to control myself. It was only after many rejections that I came to a place where I was so afraid of another rejection that I began to seek ways from and through God to help me restrain those urges to be clinging and demanding.

This was the absolute hardest part about changing because it feels like a driving force that pushes you to the limit of the other persons tolerance and maybe even beyond that limit. I reached and exceeded that limit too many times and when I did, the rejection came. I spent long hours crying out to God and shedding many tears because I did not want to go through that again. My heart hurt so badly for so many years that I went through a period of time where I prayed that God would make me numb to other people so I would not have to experience that again. I soon found out that was not the answer either.

Of all things that I could say to all those people who reached their limit with me and finally had to put their foot down and tell me "No more" I have just one thing to say even though what they did caused such intense pain, and that is: "Thank you so very much for telling me 'Enough' because had you not told me this, I would have continued imposing on you and others. Thank you from the bottom of my heart."

That is a tough one. To thank someone who has shot you through the heart and sent you packing because of your own indiscretions is very difficult, but it is the truth. I cannot thank these people enough.

For example, when a family member allows an alcoholic to call in sick knowing they have been drinking they are enabling them to continue their bad behavior, and this will go on for years. Many times the family never wises up, which lets the alcoholic continue the abuse of the substance and the family.

I was abusing my privilege of being allowed to visit by coming by without notice, calling at any time, and in any event expecting to be treated as one well respected and accepted regardless of the imposition. Those things disrupt and destroy the friendship and put strain on the married persons family. These people tolerated the impositions until they came to a place where they had to tell me it was enough. They just could not take it anymore.

So, how do you tell someone this is enough?

Well, there really is no painless easy way for a codependent person to accept the fact they are a nuisance and that they are having limits put on them. It plainly hurts and regardless of who it is, there is going to be someone who gets hurt. Too many times, it is both parties.

Unless the "imposer" restrains herself it will end up being the responsibility of the "imposee" to set the limits and from where I sit now, I have learned and am still learning to set my own limits.

From time to time Gwen will say, "I need a little help with something" which will set me on edge because I have learned that this is her lead-in to "Rose, we need some behavior modification here."

She still needs to help me along at times but I have come a long way in setting my own limits.

So the point say is this, unless the "imposer" sets her own limits, or has limits set on her, the problem probably won't go away.

In our friendship, Gwen and I both know that God has ordained our relationship. Using that as our foundation we have learned to lovingly touch each others' hearts in the good times and tough times.

If you have someone in your life who is an "imposer," and they are floating along with no restrictions on them, you are probably wondering how to approach this issue.

There are several approaches which I wish to give here that can help, but they are by no means the only avenues available.

First is the obvious direct approach, which is simply saying, "Jane, thanks for coming by but I am unable to talk now and I am sorry that I cannot invite you in. Perhaps if you call me at two-thirty this afternoon we can set up a time to have lunch." This is the quick momentary way to set a limit when you don't have time to discuss the matter.

If you have more time and you want to get to the crux of the matter you can invite them to lunch and once you have settled in to a nice conversation you can approach it something like this, "Jane, I have something that Tom and I have been discussing that I would like to share with you.

"I appreciate the fact that you are such a good friend and I enjoy your company so much but lately I have had a hard time with you dropping by unannounced. Tom gets frustrated when you do this and it cuts into his time with me. I want to continue to be your friend but you will have to prearrange a time to come by."

When you begin to speak with her about this she may get very upset as I have done. I have walked away from people who have tried to speak with me because I was trying to run away from my hurt. If they do this do not allow yourself to feel guilty. They love this because if they know you feel guilty they will use it as a tool to manipulate you and continue their behavior.

Secondly you could drop hints or have someone else talk to them which does not always work because it is easy to say, "Really! I did not know that, I really never intended to hurt anyone." Which can give the imposer some leverage to build a defense with.

Thirdly, you can buy them a book such as this one and say, "I have just read this really great book on relationships. It is about two ladies who have been friends for over ten years and how they have learned to develop a wonderful relationship." Or you could leave the book lying around your house hoping she will pick it up and read it.

Fourthly, you can write a letter.

In any of these cases, whatever you do and whichever way you decide to approach it, the very first suggestion is to ask God how He wants you do it. He knows what is most effective and how the person will take it. If the person gets offended, and never speaks to you again maybe they were not really your friend after all.

In having to accept the times Gwen has had to approach me, God has continually reminded me of my covenants with her. I have promised to be honorable, faithful, and loyal. A true friend does not take offense because God uses them to sharpen us and make us into what He wants us to be. Too many times we end up trying to ask God to make us into what we want ourselves to be and not what He wants to make of us. He uses our friends to help us come into line with what He expects.

At any rate, I would like to suggest that if you have a friend who is an "imposer," you are not doing them any favors by enabling them to sap your time and strength because they will not grow in the Lord as long as anyone allows them to maintain their inappropriate behavior.

Pray and ask God what He would have you do about this, but unless you are content with your friend and the direction of your relationship, they should not be allowed to continue with this behavior.

To the person struggling with this behavior, I sympathize with you. It is a tough place to be in but it is possible to overcome this.

There are a few things you can do to help yourself with this.

When you are the person who is struggling there is rarely a time that you feel at peace. It seems that a driving force pushes you and you are unable to stop yourself, much like an addiction. The "feeling" of that is hard to overcome, but you have to say "*No!*" to that feeling. Do not allow yourself to put faith in your feelings.

One way to start saying no is to do as I did, lie on your face before God, kick, and scream if you need to, but do it.

Isolate yourself if necessary. I have at times not answered the phone, not out of self pity, but out of determination to see this thing dead.

When the urge comes to call or stop by I would pray. I would stop and say, "I'm not doing this. God, I need help, please stop me." Give yourself fifteen minutes to stop and pray and say, "Please God, no more." If you do it enough I guarantee He will begin to take over and you will slowly begin to get control through Him, but it is impossible without Him.

Get to a Christian counselor. Professionally or through your pastor but do it away from your friend. How badly you want your friendship will determine how hard you work at it. You can't strangle your friendship and expect it to survive.

Chapter Twenty-five
My Ministry

I asked God if it would be all right with Him if I could just write a little about the times I have been privileged to pray with people for their salvation. He graciously consented.

One might ask just what does praying the Sinner's Prayer have to do with relationships. A lot.

If you are not listening to God for His prompting to pray with someone for their salvation (which is of utmost importance to Him), why would He want to bless you in other areas of your life? If you feel you are lacking in relationships, finances, talents, or just generally speaking, it may be because you have not been willing to be used to pray with someone or witness to them. This is imperative to Christian living. Others *will* go to Hell if we do not tell them. Those of us who don't tell them may go to Hell as well.

I am a Registered Nurse. One day in June 1972, I sat in a leper colony in Southeast Asia watching missionary nurses serve the poorest of earth's poor. As I watched, a great peace and sense of desire came over me to be a nurse. It would be ten years before I realized that was the moment God called me to the healing ministry. After that realization God told me that I had not just been called to help heal the body, but also to heal minds, souls, and spirits.

Perhaps the first, most moving recollection is that of a man whose condition had paralyzed him except for his eyes. He hadn't moved on his own in days. As I puttered around his room I strongly sensed God saying, "Pray with him."

So I called him by name and said that if he would be interested in praying to receive Jesus, would he blink his eyes twice. He did. Since this was a relatively new thing to me, I was a little unsure of what to say. I had only been out of nursing school a short while and had not done much witnessing previously.

I prayed the prayer of salvation over him. I felt comfortable that inside his mind, which was still active but unable to force a sound, he had repeated my prayer. When I opened my eyes, he had tears in his eyes. I noticed his hand moving under the covers, and as I reached under the sheet for his hand, something in him connected with me. After I left his room that day, I never saw him again.

A few days later as I pondered the event, I asked God, "Please tell me God, besides his salvation, what was the meaning in that precious moment?" Simply, God said, "You were his last chance." I cannot describe for you the fullness of the impact on me at that moment. To think that I was the only person who was left to tell him about Jesus. That's powerful.

At some point, I ventured to tell my preceptor about this (for I was still in orientation), and she told me firmly that it was the job of the nuns at that hospital to pray with patients and that I was not to do it again. Needless to say, I was grieved. I soon turned in my resignation.

Then there was the time two men approached me to see a particular patient. They were not relatives, nor had they ever met the man. When I asked who they were, they presented a business card from the local Assembly of God church. Their steps had been ordered by God to go to the local hospital, get on the elevator and push a certain button, get off the elevator, turn right, then left, and then to talk to the nurse.

I told them I would have to ask the patient, that I could not legally allow them into the room unless the patient agreed. So, I approached the patient. He was in a very weakened condition and was barely able to say "Yes" when I asked him if he would see these men. I asked again to make sure and he consented.

The men left before I had another chance to speak with them. This happened about half past seven.

At half past eleven I walked past the room. I had not been the nurse assigned to that room, I had just been the nurse most available to deal with the situation. As I walked past I saw the sheet pulled over the man's face and asked his nurse, "When did he die?" "About half past nine," she said.

Curious if the man had prayed, I stopped to ask God if the man had prayed to receive Jesus. God is so good to tell us things when it will boost us. Not in words, but with lots of peace, God said that he had. He had lived only two hours after praying to receive Jesus.

One of my favorite stories is about a man who had AIDS. I had gone to his room in a quiet moment to view the scene from his window.

As I stood there listening to him talk, I heard Jesus say in my right ear, "Tell him about Me." I walked to the left side of his bed and called his name and he said, "Yes?"

"What are you going to do when you get out of here?"

"Well, I am going to go home and rest and try to get better."

"I mean, where are you going when you die?"

"I'm going to Heaven. I hope."

"You don't know?"

"No."

"Do you realize you can know that you will go to Heaven?"

"Can I? Tell me how I can."

So I talked for about five minutes explaining to him why Jesus had died for him and that if he would accept Jesus he would know that he was going to Heaven when he died.

"I want to do that," he said. "I know I have lived in sin. I did wrong and I am sorry."

So I led him in the prayer of salvation and he said to me, "I have heard that same story from the priests all my life, but it never made sense to me until now when you told me."

I am so glad I listened. He died several months later.

There are many stories of people who have prayed when I felt God prompting me to pray with them. This is my calling, and what a beautiful one it has been.

Epilogue

I am sure that many of the readers of this book have at some point disagreed with much, or with part, of what I have said. That is all right. I just know that when I said I had heard God verbally speak to me and then followed through that it was the right thing to do.

At those times when I was only impressed to do or say something, and played it out, it produced good fruit.

Many people feel that God is so big and so awesome that He doesn't have to talk to us, and that because of Adam's sin He separated Himself from us never to speak to us that intimately again. Well, I have good news. God wants to be our friend, and He wants to come sit with us and talk to us. He does talk directly in one form or another at times.

Remember I said that God told me never to mistreat His creation or treat them with contempt? Well, God Himself spoke to me on that one. Jesus Himself told me to tell the AIDS patient about Him. I'm sure it was Jesus, and that Satan wouldn't send me out to be kind to God's creation or to tell a dying man about salvation.

God also communicates with us by visions. Joel 2:28-29 says, "And afterward, I will pour out My Spirit on all people. Your sons and daughters will prophesy, your old men will dream dreams, your young men will see visions. Even on both my servants, both men and women, I will pour out My Spirit in those days."

I have seen visions that have been healing to me. I was not daydreaming. They were too real. God wants to reveal Himself to us, and in these last days He is going all out to do what He has to to get our attention. We must pay attention to Him. When the time comes for Him to call us, we may not be listening or ready, as the virgins who had no oil were not ready. If we haven't learned how to hear Him, we won't know when He calls.

If you have not been exposed to some of these concepts, call on God to reveal Himself to you. You don't know what you are missing.

Should the Holy Spirit be prompting you and you feel a tugging in your heart, He may be wooing you to pray for salvation. If this is so, all you need to do is say, "Jesus, I acknowledge that I have sinned and I ask you to come into my heart and forgive me of my sin and cleanse me of all the things that have kept me from you. Please come and be Lord of my life. In Your Name, Jesus. Amen."

Bibliography

Beattie, Melody. *Codependent No More*. Center City, MN: Hazeldon Education Materials, 1987.

The NIV Study Bible, New International Version, Grand Rapids, MI. Zondervan Bible Publishers, 1985.

Webster's New Twentieth Century Dictionary of the English Language. New York. Standard Reference Works, 1957.

Music Reference

Integrity Hosanna's *Come To The Table*.

Suggested Reading List

Adult Children of Alcoholics by Janet Geringer Woititz, Ed.D
This book helps one to understand dysfunctional families and gives insight into family members of alcoholics. Can also apply to compulsive behaviors.

Beyond Codependency by Melody Beattie
A self help book to help one recover from codependency. Sequel to Codependent No More.

Covenant Relationships A Handbook for Integrity and Loyalty by Keith Intrater. Keith Intrater details Biblical principles and lays foundations for relationships both personal and in the Body of Christ as a whole helping the reader understand covenants and commitment.

Finding A Spiritual Friend How Friends And Mentors Can Make Your Faith Grow by Timothy Jones.
It is hard to know who and how to choose a spiritual mentor. Mr. Jones helps to set guidelines on what to look for in choosing a friend and mentor.

The Friendships of Women by Dee Brestin
Many times friendships are misunderstood. Dee Brestin helps the reader understand why women have deeper, more intense friendships than men.

Love Must Be Tough by James Dobson, MD
A powerful book on how to be appropriately tough and learn to respond to others without compromising your self-esteem.

The Power of a Praying Wife by Stormie Omartian
A book for women desiring a closer relationship with their husbands. Focuses on how to pray for husbands and families.

Raising Kids to Love Jesus by H. Norman Wright and Gary J. Oliver

How to communicate with and understand your children but the information is helpful in all relationships.

The Spirit-Controlled Temperament by Tim LaHaye
Understanding the personalities of others and how to relate to them in understanding and in The Holy Spirit.

The Transformation of the Inner Man by John and Paula Sandford
A detailed in depth book on inner healing.

When Your Child Wanders From God by Peter Lord
Another book on communicating and understanding others plus how to relate to your children when they stray from God.

Shattering Your Strongholds by Liberty Savard
Praying accurately in The Spirit and being able to see immediate results even when praying for and about other people. Learning to tear down those things that keep you in bondage. Learn how to set yourself free in Jesus.